DYING AND DEATH

DYING AND DEATH

Getting Rightly Prepared for the Inevitable

Joel R. Beeke

Christopher W. Bogosh

REFORMATION HERITAGE BOOKS

Grand Rapids, Michigan

Dying and Death
© 2018 by Joel R. Beeke and Christopher W. Bogosh

Reformation Heritage Books
2965 Leonard St. NE
Grand Rapids, MI 49525
616-977-0889
orders@heritagebooks.org
www.heritagebooks.org

Printed in the United States of America
18 19 20 21 22 23/10 9 8 7 6 5 4 3 2 1

Library of Congress Cataloging-in-Publication Data

Names: Beeke, Joel R., 1952- author. | Bogosh, Christopher W., author.
Title: Dying and death : getting rightly prepared for the inevitable / Joel
    R. Beeke, Christopher W. Bogosh.
Description: Grand Rapids, Michigan : Reformation Heritage Books,
    [2018] | Includes bibliographical references.
Identifiers: LCCN 2018032899 (print) | LCCN 2018043565 (ebook)
    | ISBN 9781601786517 (epub) | ISBN 9781601786500 | ISBN
    9781601786500 (paperback :alk. paper)
Subjects: LCSH: Death—Religious aspects—Christianity.
Classification: LCC BT825 (ebook) | LCC BT825 .B39 2018 (print) |
    DDC 236/.1—dc23
LC record available at https://lccn.loc.gov/2018032899

For additional Reformed literature, request a free book list from Reformation Heritage Books at the above regular or e-mail address.

Contents

With heartfelt appreciation for
Cornelis (Neil) Pronk
by God's grace,
kind and encouraging friend,
brotherly and faithful mentor,
able and Christ-centered preacher for fifty years.

—JRB

With heartfelt appreciation for
All Saints
departed and departing; or rather,
who have arrived and will one day arrive
into the embrace of the glorified Second Adam.
"Advancing still from strength to strength;
They go where other pilgrims trod,
Till each to Zion comes at length;
And stands before the face of God."
(Ps. 84:7, *The Book of Psalms for Singing*)

—CWB

Preface

Dying and death are profound, hostile, even terrifying. We all must experience an unspeakable, radical separation of our soul and body in which our soul will enter a realm fitting to its spiritual state at the moment of its final separation—that is, either heaven or hell.

Intellectually we know that dying and death are real and certain, but emotionally and spiritually we are often not able to face it. We postpone making our wills and preparing for our funerals. We find it challenging to stand beside a casket for any length of time to let the reality of death sink deep into us. Even our language betrays us: we speak of passing away or expiring rather than death. We speak of memorial parks rather than graveyards. Have you ever tried to meditate for even ten minutes on the fact that you are dying and on your inevitable death and afterlife? By nature that is nearly impossible to do. Even as Christians, it can be difficult. We can spend scores of hours planning a two-week vacation on another continent, but can scarcely spend one hour planning for a never-ending eternity.

Consequently, we do not expect this book to be a runaway best-seller! Who likes to read about dying and death? But the point of this book is that meditating on dying and death is actually profitable, even necessary, for us. We must be personally prepared to die—spiritually, ethically, and physically—so that our death will be "gain" (Phil. 1:21). To that end, Martin Luther (1483–1546) said,

"Every man must do two things alone; he must do his own believing, and his own dying."[1]

In this short book, our goal as authors has been to do three things: first, to consider the basic issues concerning our dying and death. Second, to consider Jesus's dying and death and the comfort that He can bring to us by being our Savior, Lord, and mentor in this critical area. Third, since with the advent of modern medicine and its many options for treating the body, dying and death in our modern age have become very complex, therefore, we have thought it wise to provide some facts and ethical guidance about how to approach these options.

Heartfelt thanks are in order to several people: I owe thanks to Christopher Bogosh whom I requested to be my coauthor of this book as he is much more qualified than I am to address modern medical issues related to dying and death. Basically, the parts of this book that refer to these issues were first written by him and the rest was written by me, but we have worked as a team editing each other's material. Thanks too to Misty Bourne, Ray Lanning, Gary den Hollander, and Paul Smalley for editing this book. Each of them has also made valuable contributions and suggestions. I particularly thank my colleague and Old Testament scholar, Michael Barrett, for his invaluable assistance on chapter 1. Finally, Chris and I wish to thank our dear wives, Robin and Mary, whose patience and love for our writing compulsion are appreciated far more than they know.

I dedicate this book to my good friend, Neil Pronk, who is commemorating his fiftieth anniversary of being ordained into the ministry on November 13, 1968. May God continue to abundantly bless you and your wife Ricky, Neil, as you climb in years, and grant you much continued fruitfulness in the preaching and writing work you are still being enabled to do. Thanks so much for your kind and gentle spirit, for your faithful friendship, and for being a wise mentor for so many younger ministers.

---

1. John Blanchard, comp., *The Complete Gathered Gold* (Darlington, England: Evangelical Press, 2006), 135.

Dear reader, our prayer is that God will bless this little book to help you and your loved ones prepare better for death spiritually, ethically, and physically, so as to glorify Him in both your life and your death. We are hoping that after reading it, you will be motivated to do what should be done to prepare for your passing on from this world to the next. Also, that, as a genuine Christian, you will be able to say with more assurance than ever, "For to me to live is Christ, and to die is gain" (Phil. 1:21). We also pray that those of you who are not true Christians will not rest in preparing for your death and eternity until you can say that your "only comfort in life and death [is] that I, with body and soul, both in life and death, am not my own, but belong unto my faithful Savior Jesus Christ, who, with his precious blood, has fully satisfied for all my sins, and delivered me from all the power of the devil; and so preserves me that without the will of my heavenly Father, not a hair can fall from my head; yes, that all things must be subservient to my salvation, and therefore, by his Holy Spirit, he also assures me of eternal life, and makes me sincerely willing and ready henceforth to live unto him" (Heidelberg Catechism, Q. 1).

—Joel R. Beeke

Part One

The Basics

1

DYING DEPICTED
Hope in the Old Testament

Most people do not regard dying, death, and what happens after death as pleasant subjects, but they do realize—at least deep down—that they are important. Dying, death, and judgment are the great levelers of the human race, to which we are all appointed: "it is appointed unto men once to die, but after this the judgment" (Heb. 9:27). We do not know exactly how or when we will die and enter into judgment with God, but we do know that, of all the things we think and plan about in our futures, these are "the inevitables." No wonder the Puritans used to call death, judgment, heaven, and hell, "the four last things."[1] "Appointed" in Hebrews 9:27 means *laid up* or *reserved*. This is an unavoidable appointment. It comes even to kings. Though they may live like "gods" on earth, yet the Lord says to them, "ye shall die like men" (Ps. 82:6–7).

Death comes for all of us, sooner or later. It does not ask if we are useful members of society, loving spouses and parents, obedient children, or pillars in God's church, imbued with large doses of godly piety. Death takes no bribes; it knows no denials. The appointment book is in God's hand. Your name and ours and the time and circumstances of our dying and death are all known to God (Job 14:5). He does not consult us about when we would like this appointment. Our appointment with death is unilateral not bilateral. We cannot wish this appointment away. We cannot postpone it like we can a

---

1. E.g., Robert Bolton, *The Four Last Things: Death, Judgment, Hell, and Heaven* (1632; reprint, Pittsburgh: Soli Deo Gloria, 1994).

doctor's visit. Scheduling conflicts do not figure in God's record book. In fact, we never know when it will happen.

God has a right to be in charge of your appointment with death for two simple reasons: first, because He is God; and second, because we are sinners who deserve to die. God has a right to send death our way at any moment, like a lightning bolt striking you or a thief coming to your home at night (1 Thess. 5:2). When we are young we may die; when we are old we must die. Whatever our situation at present may be, we need, therefore, to be always ready to die.

No one is so old that he does not think he has one more year to live. But none of us know whether we will live to see our next birthday; actually, we do not know whether we will see next month, or even tomorrow. All we know is that from the time when we were babies, we were sure to die. We are always moving toward death. There is but one step between death and every one of us. We are all dying people in a dying world. Many plans we make in this life never materialize, but God's plan of death will. It is the one certain thing that will happen to all of us.

Thus, two things are true of death: it is an unavoidable certainty and it will come at an unpredictable time. Pastors cannot fail to notice that even when people are close to death, their nearest relatives are still surprised at the moment when death comes.

All of this begs the ancient question: "If a man die, shall he live again?" (Job 14:14). The answer to Job's question is of great importance. The evidence of the Bible is that death is not the end of existence. The believer's hope is that being absent from the body is to be present with the Lord (2 Cor. 5:8).

Significantly, this is not uniquely a New Testament revelation. Though it is often denied by modern scholars, the Old Testament saints also had an awareness and confidence in the afterlife. Admittedly, there are not dozens of passages that deal directly with this hope in the Old Testament (as there are in the New Testament),[2]

---

2. Note that a separate chapter is not provided on the New Testament view of dying and death, as that is interwoven throughout the book.

but properly understanding some key Old Testament terms and direct statements reveals that the doctrine of life after death was a recognized truth already in Old Testament times.

Key Old Testament Words

Although it is a term associated primarily with death, *sheol* is one of the most important words in the Old Testament contributing to the doctrine of the afterlife. *Sheol* is not a happy place since it is so closely associated with death as the curse of sin. It is deep (Job 7:9), silent (Ps. 31:17), never satisfied (Prov. 27:20), associated with sorrow, distress, and anguish (Ps. 116:3), and marked by fierceness and cruelty (Song 8:6). The Authorized Version translates this word as "hell" (31 times), "grave" (31 times), and "pit" (3 times). Part of the difficulty in understanding the significance of the word is that everybody goes there, both the righteous and wicked. This is a general word that has three significant senses: (1) death in the abstract; (2) the grave; and (3) the abode or realm of departed wicked spirits. In every occurrence of the word, it is vital to identify which of the three senses is in view.

Some aspects of death do not distinguish one's spiritual condition. Both the righteous and the wicked have experienced and will experience physical death; hence, sense 1 applies to both as life ceases. The bodies of both the righteous and the wicked will decay and return to dust; hence, sense 2 also applies to both. The question is what happens after life ceases and the body corrupts. *Sheol* does indeed designate the abode of departed spirits, but there is now an important distinction between the righteous and the wicked. Whenever there is awareness or consciousness in *sheol*, it is always the wicked (for instance, Isa. 14:9); hence, sense 3 applies only to the wicked. As such, it is a place of punishment. The spirits of the righteous are never conscious or active in *sheol* for the simple reason their spirits are not there. Therefore, whenever the Scripture speaks of the righteous being in *sheol*, it is referring solely to their bodies being in the grave.

The question is: Where do the spirits of the righteous go when their bodies are in the grave? Two texts from Psalms point to the answer. Psalm 49:15 says, "But God will redeem my soul from the power of the grave; for he shall receive me." Psalm 73:24 says, "Thou shalt guide me with thy counsel, and afterward receive me to glory." The word "receive" is the clue. It occurs hundreds of times in the Old Testament, but it takes on a technical sense in the context of life after death. This sense is defined in reference to Enoch's escaping physical death: "And Enoch walked with God: and he was not; for God took (received) him" (Gen. 5:24). The text implies that God received Enoch alive directly into His presence. Similarly, in 2 Kings 2:10 Elijah described his chariot departure in the sight of Elisha as his being taken (received). Again, the text implies that God transported him alive into heaven. That the psalmists use this word expresses their belief that they would experience the same deliverance. Although they may not escape the power of death in the same manner as Enoch or Elijah, they had the same hope and expectation that God would receive them into His very presence. Significantly, after Asaph declares that God would receive him to glory, he asked a question that identifies what he means by glory: "Whom have I in heaven but thee?" (Ps. 73:25). To put it in Pauline terms, the Old Testament saint's hope was to be absent from the body and present with the Lord (2 Cor. 5:8).

Another key word is the term for "life" itself. The word, for sure, refers to physical life in contrast to physical death, but its significance goes beyond the obvious, referring to both spiritual and everlasting life. It is noteworthy that God often offered life as the blessing or motivation for obedience (see Deut. 4:1; 6:24; 8:1). To assume that the Hebrews understood this only as a longer physical life is to regard them as an extremely naïve people. The truth of the matter is that for the righteous there often comes a point that a longer physical life is no longer attractive and hardly a motive for obedience (see Job for instance). But there is more to life than just physical existence. This is clear from Wisdom's plea in Proverbs 8:35 that "whoso findeth me findeth life." This must refer to spiritual life in contrast to those who choose to remain in spiritual death (Prov. 8:36). Even more explicit is Proverbs 12:28, where the second line of the verse defines the significance of the first: "In the way of righteousness is life; and in the pathway thereof there is no death." Here, "life" equates to "no death," that is, to immortality. It is not true that the righteous are exempt from physical death, but they do possess a life that is everlasting. This was David's hope when he confessed that he would dwell in the house of God (in His presence) forever (Ps. 23:6). It is indeed the hope of every believer when walking through that inevitable valley of death's shadow.

Key Old Testament Texts
Understanding the key words expands the number of Old Testaments texts that address the issue of life after death. We will focus on three passages that are explicit in expressing the hope of life beyond death.

Job 19:25–27 is one of those passages: "For I know that my redeemer liveth, and that he shall stand at the latter day upon the earth: and though after my skin worms destroy this body, yet in my flesh shall I see God: whom I shall see for myself, and mine eyes shall behold, and not another." There is some question as to whether Job's confession refers to his confidence of life in the intermediate state or to his hope in the resurrection, but there is no question that he is sure that his present suffering life was not the end. His confidence was that his Redeemer would sooner or later stand upon the earth (literally, dust, most likely referring to his grave) for his vindication and that in his flesh he would see God. The statement "in his flesh" is open to interpretation. The Hebrew preposition is usually translated "from." It could mean "apart from" his flesh he would see God, a reference to the intermediate state in which he would be without a body in God's presence. Or it could mean "from the vantage point" of his flesh, a reference to a future bodily resurrection since his current body would be decayed in the grave. The resurrection idea is better, but either way there is hope of continuing life for the believer.

Isaiah 26:19 is one of the most direct prophecies concerning the resurrection: "Thy dead men shall live, together with my dead body shall they arise. Awake and sing, ye that dwell in dust: for thy dew is as the dew of herbs, and the earth shall cast out the dead." The pronouns suggest the prophet especially has in view the bodily resurrection of the righteous (note that Isaiah 24:22 may refer to the resurrection of the wicked). Significantly, the imperative "awake" also occurs in resurrection contexts, such as in Psalm 17:15: "As for me, I will behold thy face in righteousness: I shall be satisfied, when I awake, with thy likeness." Packed in this verse is the hope of resurrection (awake), glorification (with God's likeness), and eternal bliss (satisfied).

Finally, Daniel 12:2 predicts the resurrection: "Many of them that sleep in the dust of the earth shall awake, some to everlasting life, and some to shame and everlasting contempt." The language is explicit, revealing that there will be a resurrection of both the righteous and the wicked. Not only does the text express the certainty of the bodily resurrection, it also contrasts the eternal fates of the righteous and wicked. Some will be raised to "everlasting life" and some to "shame and everlasting contempt." Daniel's language anticipates what John designated as the "first resurrection" and "the second death" (Rev. 20:5–15).

Though abundantly clear in the New Testament, the sobering realization that man will live someplace forever is already clear in the Old Testament. It is a solid hope and living comfort for God's people to know that death has lost its sting and is for them the doorway to glory and to being with God forever. It is a warning to unbelievers that death's sting will only intensify as they are sentenced to that second, never-ending death of eternal torment. It is incumbent on the living to flee to the ever-living Redeemer, Jesus Christ, whom to know is life eternal (John 17:3). Where one lives in eternity depends on how one lives in time (John 3:36; 5:28–29; Rev. 20:12).

2

DYING DEMYSTIFIED
Facts about Death

There is a remarkable difference between how an unbeliever and a believer look at dying, death, and the afterlife. For the unbeliever or the agnostic, death is mysterious and the afterlife is even more dubious. For the believer, death is not an extinction or a terminus but only a transition, a junction. Though solemn, it is demystified in Christ and the afterlife is the best life. Let's consider this contrast.

After Death—Agnosticism's Version
Sally, the hospice nurse, stood by Bruno's bedside.[1] Bruno was a prisoner with amyotrophic lateral sclerosis (ALS), who had been transferred to the hospital with his fifth bout of pneumonia in the past six months.[2] He was serving a life sentence for the murder of his elderly neighbor, who had attempted to stop him from stealing his narcotic pain medications. While incarcerated, he developed ALS, underwent a tracheotomy, and became dependent on a ventilator to breathe.[3] Bruno had a choice: return to prison on the ventilator

---

1. Most names and identifying details were changed throughout this book to protect anonymity.

2. Also referred to as Lou Gehrig's disease, ALS is a debilitating disease of the nervous system. As the condition progresses, people lose their ability to control muscle movements which causes problems with speaking, eating, and breathing. The ability to think is not lost, however.

3. As the musculature degrades in people with ALS, a surgical incision in the neck (tracheotomy) and a machine to cause the mechanics of respiration (ventilator) are required, if breathing is to be sustained; increased respiratory

until suffering the next bout of pneumonia with the possibility of dying by suffocation; or, have the ventilator withdrawn, receiving medications to manage his respiratory distress, and dying in the luxury of a hospice facility. Needless to say, Bruno, who thought he was the victim of injustice, did not like his choices.

As he lay silent with expressive eyes, paralyzed, his right wrist handcuffed to the bedrail, and a prison guard by his side, Sally presented her case for hospice care: "Bruno, I know this is a difficult choice to make, but we will keep you comfortable after the ventilator is removed. You won't have to go back to prison—you won't suffer anymore."

Sally was presenting the common view that what happens after death is in some way better than persisting in this present state, even for unrepentant murderers who see themselves as victims of the system. In Europe and America, it is quite acceptable to choose or create a self-customized hereafter. If one wants to believe in nirvana, reincarnation, a happy hunting ground, heaven, any combination of these possibilities, or else simple annihilation, the modernist will not object—provided the belief is not imposed on others. According to the modern mindset, no one really knows what happens after death. "What is emphatically clear is that everyone is dying, and one day, we will all die," says the modernist, "so why not permit the imagination to wander when it comes to the hereafter?"

For many centuries the church was the predominant institution addressing dying, death, and what happens after death, not hospices and medical institutions that could be indifferent to or at odds with traditional Christianity. Following the beginning of the scientific age in the seventeenth century, the medicalization of death in the nineteenth century, and the increasing effectiveness of medical science in the decades that followed, the church was pushed aside. A paradigm shift occurred. The church is now on the periphery and modern medicine has shifted to the center. Moving into

---

secretions and the individual's inability to clear them usually results in repeated episodes of fluid in the lungs (pneumonia).

the twentieth century, many hospitals in the West, once Christian institutions in purpose, ethics, and practice, have become Christian in name only. Influenced by the rise of higher criticism, liberal theology, and the social gospel, these hospitals no longer affirm a supernatural-natural Christ-centered worldview grounded in Holy Scripture. In the twenty-first century, modern medicine is eager to fill the void left by the traditional, confessional, and biblical church.

Since the two absolutes of dying and death have become medicalized—that is, as aspects of human experience to be addressed by doctors and nurses rather than by ministers of the Word or one's fellow Christians—it is not surprising to see health-care professionals, like Sally, asserting an unqualified view of what happens after death to provide answers, comfort, and hope. This position is commonly referred to as agnosticism, which is derived from the Greek *agnosis* meaning "a state of unknowing," that is, with respect to metaphysical questions such as the existence of God or an afterlife. Thus, an agnostic claims not to know matters beyond his or her ability to observe or quantify them. This approach to empirical or scientific facts has the appearance of humility. As a philosophical system, however, agnosticism is a proud and unconditional assertion in which all that can be known with certainty must be measured, tested, demonstrated, and verified by hands-on experience. Agnosticism is an outright rejection of non-empirical truth, which claims, *without empirical validation,* the impossibility of knowing truth outside the process of scientific investigation!

Two major issues stand behind agnosticism in the contemporary West: pluralism and the eventual failure of medical science to sustain life. In western democracies, citizens have a right to believe what they choose, so long as they do not act on their beliefs in violation of civil law and they tolerate other people's beliefs. All of these personal views address the hereafter in some way, so agnosticism provides a vehicle for tolerance and affirmation.

Another primary factor already alluded to is the innate human need for answers, comfort, and hope. Dying and death are absolute—we are dying, and one day we will cease to be as we are now. This is mysterious, uncomfortable, and even dreadful. Someday medical science will fail us, when the doctor says he can do no more for us. After all the optimistic counsel from well-meaning healthcare professionals and hopeful state-of-the-art medical treatments, dying and death stand firm and fixed on our human agendas—then what? In modern medical practice a referral to hospice is made, and end-of-life experts come alongside to support individualized answers, provide comfort in the midst of suffering, and affirm one's self-customized hopes for some good or life after death. ˒

Death as a Natural Part of Life

In a similar way, modern medicine commonly promotes the view that death is a natural and normal part of human existence. Since dying is a process running parallel with life, in modern medicine the death of the body has become associated with the outworking of natural laws of life. In medical literature, one will often find dying and death associated with pregnancy and birth, or as a stage in a natural process, much like a caterpillar emerging from a cocoon as a butterfly. This interpretation is rooted in the rise of evolutionary biology in the late nineteenth century. According to this viewpoint, no line exists between dying and the death of the body, because they are both the outworking of natural laws of survival occurring in the larger cycle of life. Thus, people facing death should accept and even welcome death with optimism as a transition to a self-customized hereafter.

These naturalistic and evolutionary theories have also prevailed in modern medicine to define death. To determine the moment when life ceases and death occurs, doctors today speak of "brain death," the point at which, in the judgment of the attending physician, "worthwhile activity" ceases in the three pounds of biochemical tissue in the skull. According to modern medicine's definition of death, an individual may have a beating heart, a level of integrative function between the brain and body, and the continuation of cellular processes in the body indicating life, but the person may still be pronounced dead. The residual signs of life are interpreted as mere operations of the laws of nature that will not sustain the ongoing survival of a human person as a whole. Contrary to popular belief, biblically informed medical science has proven that we are more than biochemical substances bent on survival; dying and death are not natural and normal parts of life; there is in fact a distinct line separating dying from living, and even the death of the body from its life.

Dying and the Death of the Body—the Facts

We may learn a true view of physical death by studying the word of God. Although the Holy Scriptures are not a book of science, they do provide a basic framework to understand life and death— a framework within which we can accurately view the findings of science. The Bible teaches us that human life is a creation and gift of God: "And the Lord God formed man of the dust of the ground, and breathed into his nostrils the breath of life; and man became a living soul" (Gen. 2:7). An essential element of our life is "breath," a quality that man shares with the animals (Gen. 7:21–22). The Bible also closely associates "blood" with life, going so far as to say that the life of a man or beast is in the blood (Gen. 9:4–5; Lev. 17:11, 14; Deut. 12:23). Consequently, "blood" can represent violence and death (Gen. 4:10–11). Death itself is God's judgment upon sin (Gen. 2:17), a doctrine to which we will return in a later chapter. God pronounced that judgment in these words: "In the sweat of thy face shalt thou eat bread, till thou return unto the ground; for out of it wast thou taken: for dust thou art, and unto dust shalt thou return" (Gen. 3:19). Therefore, life is found in the breath and blood of the body, and death is marked by the decomposition of the body into the earth from which God formed it.

Medical *science* also identifies the physical death of a human being with the end of cardiopulmonary activity (breath and blood) and the onset of decomposition (to dust). These set an observable

boundary dividing the state of physical life from the state of death.
When the heart, lungs, and circulatory system cease to distrib-
ute oxygen throughout the body, there is a change from aerobic
(oxygen-fueled) action in the body to anaerobic (non-oxygen
fueled) activity, which is referred to as corruption or decomposition. During decomposition, autolysis or self-digestion starts. As the
temperature of the body continues to decrease, rigor mortis (stiff-
ness of limbs) sets in. About four days later, putrefaction begins. It is
interesting to note that Jesus lay in the grave for three days without
corruption (Ps. 16:10; Acts 2:27) and Lazarus for four with sus-
pected putrefaction (John 11:39). During putrefaction, foul-smelling
methane, hydrogen sulfide, and ammonia fumes are released from
rotting tissues, the body liquefies, and eventually the entire body
dissolves or disintegrates—"unto dust shalt thou return" (Gen.
3:19). The death of the human body, then, is not merely the death of
certain cells in it. On a microscopic level, cells are constantly dying
in our bodies. Nor is it the death of an organ in the body. Medically
speaking, death comes from the systemic disruption of cardiopulmonary activity such that oxygen-based life processes are replaced
by a process of decay into earth.

Since the 1980s it has become common to certify a person's
death by the end of measurable brain activity, a condition commonly referred to as "brain death." As noted above, both the Bible
and a basic scientific understanding of death focus on the end of
breathing, but the invention of the ventilator blurred this definition.
Thus, it is possible for a nonresponsive person to have no detectable
brain activity and for the air-pumping machine to aerate the lungs.
This mechanical process provides the heart with oxygen-rich blood
to keep it beating, which in turn circulates the blood throughout
the body. While the heart can initiate an impulse to beat without
the brain, the lungs require a stimulus from the brain, more specifically the brain-stem, in order for them to function. The ventilator
bypasses this physiological process, and rather than just removing
the non-responsive person from the life-sustaining apparatus to
see if breathing stops, and soon after the beating heart, the medical

community has adopted brain-death criteria to certify death. This legal move enables the procurement of healthy organs from "brain-dead" donors.[4] At least two serious matters may be raised about defining death in such a manner.

First, "brain death" is often ambiguous and poorly defined. To what extent must the brain be inactive for it to be considered "dead"? Aside from the beating heart, it is necessary to point out that a level of activity still occurs between parts of the brain and body, which indicates the brain is not truly dead according to brain-death criteria which in the United States is "irreversible cessation of *all* parts of the brain" (italics ours). It is well documented that when a surgeon cuts into a "brain-dead" organ donor, heart rate and blood pressure increase, which indicates a physiological interaction between the brain and organs in the body. This is a common stress response on the heart occurring along the hypothalamic, pituitary, and adrenal axis (HPA axis). The hypothalamus is a region in the brain, the pituitary gland is a structure at the base of the brain, and the adrenal glands are on the top of the kidneys in the body; and this physiological pathway modulates heart rate and blood pressure. "Brain-death" can be a dangerous definition of death insofar as it can prove expedient to justify acts that terminate a still-living human body, perhaps to harvest its organs.

Second, those who believe that human life begins at the cellular level contradict themselves if they define life by brain activity. One cannot be consistent in believing that life begins at conception (i.e., the time when a male sperm penetrates a female's egg and a separate human life starts at the cellular level) and accept brain death as a valid definition of death since the nervous system and brain do not develop until five to six weeks after conception. If one sees brain-death as a valid definition of death, then why not permit abortion at least until the latter half of the first trimester of pregnancy? This is not merely a human being "in potential,"

---

4. See Elaine Chen, "The Complex Intersection between Critical Care and Palliative Care," *AHA Media: A Relias Learning Company* (September 1, 2015).

but, according to Holy Scripture, he or she is a unique developing person with a God-breathed, life-giving spirit animating a distinct cellular structure in a woman's womb (cf. Gen. 2:7; Ps. 139:13–16; Luke 1:13, 30–36, 41–44).

Biblical Conclusions

Biblically informed medical science proves the death of the body is not a natural aspect of life or a necessary concomitant to it and brain death can be a dangerous way to define the boundary between life and death. Agnosticism about what happens after physical death is indefensible, for Holy Scripture is emphatically clear: "For we must all appear before the judgment seat of Christ; that every one may receive the things done in his body, according to that he hath done, whether it be good or bad. Knowing therefore the terror of the Lord, we persuade men" (2 Cor. 5:10–11). "*Knowing* therefore... we persuade men" (italics ours). What is known? The "fear of the Lord" as the Judge of the whole human race! All will "appear," body and soul, "before the judgment seat of Christ" to account for every thought, word, and deed done while living.

Finally, contrary to the false hopes encouraged by agnostic modern thought and modern medicine, the death of the body is only the beginning of sorrows for those who have been so foolish as to live apart from God and continue in sin. After death there is a day of judgment slated on the calendar of God; all must appear before His tribunal, and none shall be spared (2 Cor. 5:10). Death is an enemy, but Christ overcame death by His own resurrection from death, and has robbed death of its sting or power to hurt those who belong to Christ (1 Cor. 15:54–57). Ultimately, He will destroy death itself, raising the dead from their graves and summoning all human beings to appear before His judgment seat. Those who in this life were joined to Him by a true faith will be acknowledged by Him and received into the glory and life of heaven. Those who hardened their hearts and went on in their sins will be condemned by Him and cast out into the horrible darkness and everlasting burnings of hell. Such is the future of the human race according to the plan of God revealed in His word.

While agnostics claim that what may follow death is mysterious and nothing can be known about it for certain, those who receive the Holy Scriptures as the true and trustworthy account of the will of God for our salvation, have a sure and certain knowledge about these things. Thus, the Scriptures expose and refute the errors of agnosticism and modern medicine, demystifying their view of death, and giving hope to those who trust in Christ alone for the victory over death that their Savior grants.

3

DYING DEFINED
The Wages of Sin

Death is not a debt to nature, but is God's judgment upon sin. Rhode Island's first attorney general, William Dyer (1609–c. 1677), wrote: "Were it not for sin, death had never had a beginning, and were it not for death, sin would never have had an ending." The famous Puritan commentator, Matthew Henry (1662–1714), said, "Death is as due to a sinner as wages are to a servant."[1] Paul said it best of all: "The wages of sin is death" (Rom. 6:23).

Creation and Providence
When I (Christopher Bogosh) was a theological student, I attended First Reformed Presbyterian Church in Cambridge, Massachusetts. Many who attended this church were post-graduate students pursuing doctorates at Harvard University and the Massachusetts Institute of Technology (MIT). Others were post-doctorate professionals working in the greater Boston area. The church was literally a think tank and, for one who bloomed late as a student, the atmosphere was downright intimidating!

My years at Cambridge were formative for my thinking about dying. During a discussion with a member at the church, I mentioned that death was not present before the fall of mankind. After all, the Bible teaches that "the wages of sin is death" was the result of sin (Rom. 6:12). The member replied: "What about the vegetation Adam and Eve ate? Plants had to die to feed them."

---

1. Cited in Blanchard, *Complete Gathered Gold*, 138.

"Good point," I replied, and changed the topic.

As I dug deeper into this subject, I found it quite complex, especially in light of the findings of medical science about the human body. God gave Adam and Eve permission to eat vegetation or fruit from the garden (Gen. 2:16), and as the church member had pointed out, this required the death of living plants. Further, in digestion, the nutrients from dead vegetation are broken down into molecular components the body can use to sustain life. Medical science has also proven that cellular death occurs in the human body to promote the continuation of life. For example, our body replaces its skin or epithelial cells about once a month. Old cells die and are sloughed off and new ones emerge. Additionally, the molecular structure of the entire body changes and is renewed about every ten years! At the cellular level, our old physical body is ever dying and a new one comes to life. Obviously, my previous thinking about death before the Fall was too simplistic.

The solution to the problem of death before the Fall is found in how God has chosen to create human beings and how He has chosen to continue their existence through His providential laws. God's laws consistently operate both before and after the Fall according to the way He has determined. Theologians refer to this as the decree of God, which is the triune Creator's eternal, infinite, unchangeable, all-powerful, and omni-dimensional plan for His creation. Just as an architect has a plan to build a house in all its many details before he has it built, God has a plan with everything predetermined, including all of its cause-and-effect relationships. All of the subatomic particles and spiritual entities that will ever exist are included in the decree, as well as all of the providential laws that will govern their intended form, activity, arrangement, and ongoing existence.

After God created the components that constitute human bodies and the necessary elements to promote their survival, no new "stuff" from outside of God's original creation was necessary. "In the beginning God created the heaven and the earth" (Gen. 1:1). "For in him we live, and move, and have our being," and the triune Creator is "upholding all things by the word of his power"

(Acts 17:28; Heb. 1:3). Further, everything God created was "good"; indeed it was "very good" (Gen. 1:31). The Hebrew word translated "good" has a wide range of meanings depending on context; here it refers especially to excellence, wholeness, and perfection. The original creation so delighted God as to evoke His blessing, and moved Him to cease from His labors and enter into rest as the Maker of all things. What God had created satisfied His purposes, so He chooses providentially to uphold it and to direct it to fulfill His will in time and space. This includes the ongoing propagation of humans from the sixth day on as natural-supernatural beings: "God formed man of the dust of the ground, and breathed into his nostrils the breath of life; and man became a living soul" (Gen. 2:7).

God will not permit what He has created to be annihilated—death never equals the non-existence of a human being. What ultimately exists in the physical universe is either matter or energy that is constantly recycled but never totally obliterated, because God chooses to sustain them by His omnipotent hand. Of course, as creatures of God, matter and energy are not eternal. Their existence depends on the eternal triune Creator who made, upholds, and governs them every moment according to providential laws and predestined ends.

Apoptosis
Concerning human cells, a process called *apoptosis* occurs to achieve material change in the body. According to Lauralee Sherwood, author of the medical textbook, *Human Physiology: from Cells to Systems*, the cells in the human body receive "a constant stream of 'survival signals', which reassure the cell that it is useful to the body"; if these signals are not received, they "are programmed to commit suicide."[2] Via apoptosis, which actually means "a process of falling away or dropping off" and not "suicide," human cells die as a means to achieve survival of the body. Apoptosis occurs in the

---

2. Lauralee Sherwood, *Human Physiology: from Cells to Systems*, 7th ed. (Belmont, Calif.: Brooks/Cole, 2007), 125.

early stages of *in utero* development to structure the body, it continues outside the womb to facilitate growth, and it serves during aging to remove unnecessary cells. This process is a providential law of life ordained by the triune Creator that operated before the Fall and continues to operate afterwards.

Necrosis

After the Fall, however, cellular processes had the potential to be harmful to the body. "Considering that every cell's life hangs in delicate balance at all times," writes Sherwood, "it is not surprising that faulty control of apoptosis—resulting in either too much or too little cell suicide—appears to participate in many major diseases."[3] At the cellular level, this type of death is referred to as *necrosis*. It is not a "natural law of life" as biological evolution suggests. Contrasting necrosis with apoptosis, Sherwood writes: "In necrosis the dying cells are passive victims, whereas in apoptosis the cells actively participate in their own deaths."[4] Aside from the immediate destruction or mortal wounding of the human body, much physical death after the Fall results from defective apoptosis and/or active necrosis at the cellular level.

Sin and Dying

While cellular "death" by apoptosis to promote life was present in Eden, necrosis and the physical death of a human being were not. Dying is a post-Fall phenomenon running parallel and competing with living until it overcomes the body, causing us to return to dust. Indeed, "the wages of sin is death," but in a more radical sense, which will be considered in greater depth in the next chapter, "Dying Delayed," sin disrupted the creation and brought down the triune Creator's providential curse (Genesis 3). Sin resulted in the appointment of physical death for Adam, Eve, and their

---

3. Sherwood, *Human Physiology*, 125.
4. Sherwood, *Human Physiology*, 124.

descendants (Gen. 2:9, 17). Sin caused death to enter the experience of human life (see the refrain in Genesis 5, "and he died"). Physical death is not the result of the operation of the laws of life, but occurs when the unnatural process of dying overtakes and overwhelms the operation of those laws.

Ecclesiastes 12:1–8 describes the post-Fall decay caused by dying as we age. This passage is an extended metaphor or simile likening the body and the process of aging to everyday things and events in the ancient Middle East. The aging body is like a house falling into a state of disrepair. Hair turns white. Arms and legs develop weakness and tremors. Musculoskeletal deformities occur, and walking becomes difficult. Teeth rot, lips sink into the mouth, and it is difficult to chew food. Problems with eyesight develop. Worries and anxieties trouble the mind, resulting in light sleep and darkened moods. Sexual impotence occurs. Suffering and loss are experienced, and death is just around the corner. The "silver cord" is ready to be loosed, and the "golden bowl" is set to be broken (Eccl. 12:6).

Dying by disease was also caused by sin. The Holy Scriptures and literature from every culture, age, time, and place contain descriptions of this miserable reality. There are afflictions from the outside, such as *mycobacterium leprae*, the bacterium that causes leprosy, and a whole host of unseen viruses and toxins in the environment that accelerate dying. These are diseases caused by an exterior source, however, sin has also, pierced to the depths of our genes and caused diseases to occur from within. These are disorders of a genetic and biochemical nature—congenital birth defects, auto-immune disorders, and cancers, to name a few major categories.[5]

---

5. These tragic conditions are caused by a disordered sequencing of genes in the human genome. Children born with congenital birth defects may have gross malformations of the body and lack the ability to interact with the environment. People with autoimmune disorders have immune systems that attack their own bodies. Individuals with cancer possess replicating cells that cause tumors to invade and erode healthy organs and tissue.

Assaults from inside and outside the body may be acute or chronic, causing death to occur in a matter of days or over a much longer period of time.

Then too there is self-inflicted acceleration of dying because we act sinfully. A large measure of the physical decline we experience is due to destructive sinful behaviors, such as gluttony, anger, and laziness. Many diseases are not a normal part of aging, that is, "in the genes" or due to the environment; they are caused by sinful living. Sin has made us our own worst enemies by causing us to harm ourselves! Thus, sin separates us from God, a cursed creation surrounds us with hostile forces bent on our destruction, and we bring down the heavy hand of death on ourselves. Truly, "the wages of sin is death."

Spiritual and Eternal Death

Death is ultimately undefinable. The reality of felt separation that it conveys when we lose our loved ones goes far beyond words. The word "separation," therefore, must lie at the heart of our feeble attempts to define death. Physical death is the separation of the soul from the body. But that is not all there is to death, since our physical death is never the end of our existence. The Bible also speaks of two kinds of death that are far worse: spiritual death and eternal death. These two kinds of death are also the wages of sin.

Spiritual death is the separation of the soul from God's favor. That happened instantaneously to Adam in Paradise when he fell into sin. That is how we are born by nature as fallen sons and daughters of sin, separated from God in our soul though receiving benefits from God for our bodies. David put it this way: "Behold, I was shapen in iniquity; and in sin did my mother conceive me" (Ps. 51:5). And Paul wrote to the Ephesians, "And you hath he quickened, who were dead in trespasses and sins" (Eph. 2:1). That is why Jesus said of everyone who is born into this world: "Ye must be born again" (John 3:7).

Eternal death is the separation of a person's soul and body from God forever in hell. Hell is a final and irreversible state (Luke 16:25–26) of punishment (Matt. 25:46), torment (Mark 9:44), destruction (2 Thess. 1:9), imprisonment (Jude 6), as well as darkness, grief, and pain (Matt. 8:12). In eternal death, those justly condemned to hell do not even experience the common mercies of God that the unbeliever experiences in this life; the wrath of God is poured out without mixture upon the damned forever (Rev. 14:10–11). In hell, the damned are ever dying but never fully physically dead even as they remain under spiritual and eternal death—without intermission, without a second chance, without annihilation, and without end (Isa. 33:14; Matt. 25:41; Jude 8). Truly, "the wages of sin is death"—physical death, spiritual death, eternal death.

Thank God that Romans 6:23 goes on to say, "but the gift of God is eternal life through Jesus Christ our Lord." Astonishingly, Jesus Christ bore the essence of this threefold death on Calvary's cross as a substitute for sinners such as we are: on the cross, He underwent physical death when He "bowed his head, and gave up the ghost" (John 19:30); He bore the essence of spiritual death when He cried out, "My God, my God, why hast thou forsaken me?" (Matt. 27:46); and He bore the essence of eternal death when "He descended into hell" (Apostles' Creed, art. 4) "by His inexpressible anguish, pains, terrors, and hellish agonies, in which He was plunged during all His sufferings, but especially on the cross, [by which He] has delivered me from the anguish and torments of hell" (Heidelberg Catechism, Q. 44).

Behold the mystery of the gospel! The sinless Son of God bore "the wages of sin" so that you, dear believer, could be set free when you, by grace, repent before Him and believe in Him alone for salvation. He bore your sin through suffering the essence of this dreadful threefold death so that you could live forever for the sake of Christ's righteousness. Paul captures this wondrous gospel in a nutshell in 2 Corinthians 5:21: "For he [God the Father] hath made him [Jesus Christ] to be sin for us, who knew no sin; that we might be made the righteousness of God in him." Reflecting on this, the Puritan

Elisha Coles (c. 1608–1688) wrote, "Sin could not die, unless Christ died; Christ could not die, without being made sin; nor could He die, but sin must die with Him."[6]

Through this substitutionary obedience of Christ, you not only can be saved, but you can have eternal life: "This is life eternal, that they might know thee the only true God, and Jesus Christ, whom thou hast sent" (John 17:3). In Christ you can find deliverance from spiritual and eternal death, and even your physical death will serve ultimately only as a passageway into eternal life. The prolific Puritan Thomas Watson (c. 1620–1686) wrote, "Death breaks the union between the body and the soul but perfects the union between Christ and the soul."[7] In Christ you will receive a life of joy, abundance, peace, purpose, and fulfilment. By bearing "the wages of sin" for you, He turns death into life—forever!

---

6. H. J. Horn, comp., *The Puritans Day by Day* (1928; repr., Edinburgh: Banner of Truth, 2016), 173.

7. Horn, *The Puritans Day by Day*, 132.

4

DYING DELAYED
The Grace of Medicine

We are blessed to have the medical care we do today. We have witnessed many people's lives being prolonged through God blessing surgeries and medicines that were not available even a few decades ago. But as with all the best blessings, they are easy to idolize. The Heidelberg Catechism (Q. 95) says, "Idolatry is, instead of, or besides that one true God who has manifested Himself in His Word, to contrive, or have any other object, in which men place their trust."[1] It is all too easy to believe and end in the gifts of medicine rather than in the Giver of the gifts.

We are convinced that many Christians in the West are putting their trust more in medicine than in God. This is one of the major issues facing the church in the twenty-first century. For example, in our professions as a healthcare worker and pastors, we have met many Christians who pursue every medical treatment possible to avoid death, even when the potential cure causes significant harm to the body, wreaks havoc in the lives of others, and the treatments challenge biblical commands.[2] When medical care is approached from this perspective, it is in opposition to a Christian worldview and, more importantly, it is a poor testimony to Christ's victory over death and dying.

---

1. *The Three Forms of Unity*, ed. Joel R. Beeke (Birmingham, Ala.: Solid Ground Christian Books, 2010), 102.

2. For a helpful, balanced view of this subject, see Bill Davis, *Departing in Peace: Biblical Decision-making at the End of Life* (Phillipsburg, N.J.: P&R, 2017).

In our modern culture, medical science has an extremely powerful hold on people, because it is possible to replicate effective treatment to slow dying and even, in some cases, to reverse it. "Overtreatment" and "undertreatment" are both modern problems; that is to say, not using reasonable means to prolong life or prolonging one's life at all costs may actually become an idol when it conflicts with doing God's will ("what is right").[3]

There are three views of death in our culture. The first view regards death as natural and it should be sought and embraced. This often leads to abandoning life prematurely—that is, to "undertreatment." The second view regards death as a disaster that must be avoided at all costs. This view often leads to making physical life the highest good of life, that is, life itself has more intrinsic value than anything else. This view sees little or no redeemable qualities in suffering and does everything possible to keep everyone alive to the last possible moment at all times regardless of the emotional, spiritual, and financial cost. The result is often "overtreatment." The third view regards death as a real evil, the result of man's moral rebellion, while also recognizing that death can be conquered by means of God's triumphant grace in Jesus Christ. This view understands that Christians embrace real victory in death, such that even death cannot separate them from the love of God in Jesus Christ (Rom. 8:38–39). The result of this view is usually "proper treatment" that avoids both "undertreatment" and "overtreatment."

Death Is a State, Dying Is a Process

According to Holy Scripture, sin is the most fundamental cause of death along with all the other miseries of this life, including alienation from the tree of life and the living God. This is a problem medical science cannot treat. Here we must distinguish between

---

3. See John F. Kilner, "Forgoing Treatment," in *Dignity and Dying: A Christian Appraisal,* ed. John F. Kilner, Arlene B. Miller, and Edmund D. Pellegrino (Grand Rapids: Eerdmans, 1996), 69–83, for a balanced approach between "overtreatment" and "undertreatment."

sin and misery; that is, between Adam's sinful disobedience and its consequences for him and all of his descendants. Misery is a good confessional term[4] for everything wrong with this life, including, most importantly, alienation from God, one's fellow humans, and even from oneself. Medical science cannot reconcile sinners to God, but it can mitigate some of the physical and emotional consequences of the fall.

The first transgression Adam committed was the sin that cast all of us into a *state* of death. "Wherefore," writes Paul, "as by one man sin entered into the world, and death by sin; and so death passed upon all men, for that all have sinned" (Rom. 5:12). Sin and death are imputed to us through Adam's fall, and they now spread like an unstoppable Ebola virus to the entire human race. We all transgressed, we all sinned, and we all died with Adam in his first sin. In the Garden of Eden, Eve was deceived by Satan, but it was not until she gave some fruit "unto her husband with her; and he did eat," that sin, dying, and death entered the human experience (Gen. 3:6; cf. 1 Tim. 2:13). In Adam the entire human race "died" (1 Cor. 15:22); the essence of this death is estrangement from the living, triune Creator and banishment from Eden's tree of life (Gen. 3:22–24).

Spiritual Death

Sinners are dead even while they are alive. This condition is referred to as spiritual death and Psalm 88 describes the state: "I am counted with them that go down into the pit: I am as a man that hath no strength: Free among the dead, like the slain that lie in the grave, whom thou rememberest no more: and they are cut off from thy hand" (vv. 4–5). Though ultimately this psalm is a prophetic account of Christ in His sufferings, some commentators believe

---

4. E.g., see the first section of the Heidelberg Catechism on "The Misery of Man" (Lord's Days 2–4), and the Westminster Shorter Catechism, Q. 19: "What is the misery of that estate whereinto man fell?" A. "All mankind by their fall lost communion with God, are under his wrath and curse, and so made liable to all miseries in this life, to death itself, and to the pains of hell forever."

Psalm 88 was written by a leper—a diseased person who thinks he is cursed by God and whom the healthy ostracize (cf. Lev. 13:46). According to this leper, the spiritually dead are those appointed to the grave, who abide under God's wrath (Ps. 88:7), and who are alienated from the community of the living (v. 8). This is the state of those estranged from the living God, whom Paul describes as "having no hope, and without God in the world" (Eph. 2:12). An individual dying in a state of spiritual death has an appointment with physical death and he or she will go "down into the pit" after death to partake of eternal death (v. 4). This is what Holy Scripture calls the "second death" (Rev. 21:8).

The Second Death
The phrase "second death" is used four times in the Bible, each occurring in the book of Revelation (Rev. 2:11; 20:6, 14; 21:8). Thus, there can be no agnosticism about what happens after the spiritually dead die. When unbelievers die the first death, the death of the body, their bodies return to the earth while their souls go to their Creator who commits them to hell. Their second death is their final state when, following the reuniting of their souls and bodies in the resurrection, they are brought before the tribunal of God where they will be judged, condemned, and cast into hell. That is a place separate from the blessings of God, where, under the wrath of God, they will experience continual suffering in both body and soul forever. In hell dying continues unabated without relief from pain, suffering, and misery forever. The graces of medicine are a bygone mercy as the spiritually dead enter the state of eternal death or the "second death," without the grace of salvation and the hope of everlasting healing, living, and life. The great preacher, Charles Spurgeon, explained the unbeliever's state after physical death like this: "Lost to God, lost to heaven, lost to time, lost to the preaching of the Gospel, lost to the invitation of mercy, lost to the prayers of

the gracious, lost to the mercy seat, lost to the blood of sprinkling, lost to all hope of every sort—lost, lost, forever."[5]

Jesus used the maggot-infested, burning garbage pit in the Hinnom Valley near Jerusalem as an illustration to describe the second death (Mark 9:48). At this desecrated location, child sacrifices had been offered to Molech (2 Kings 23:10). Jesus described the future destiny of the wicked as a perpetual experience of "darkness"—one characterized by "weeping and gnashing of teeth" (Matt. 8:12). We cannot begin to fathom the horrors of the "second death," but the Holy Scriptures are clear about the reality of its existence and the miserable experience the never-annihilated and fully-conscious spiritually dead will have there. Unbelievers are barred from true living, the tree of life, and the joyful presence of the triune Creator. They are given over completely, body and soul, to their desired alienation from the living God into everlasting condemnation in hell. This is the second death.

The Grace of Medicine—Dying Delayed

After Adam and Eve disregarded God's warning, "thou shalt surely die" (Gen. 2:17) and ate the forbidden fruit, spiritual death entered creation, along with two divine appointments: the day of one's physical death and the day of one's experience of the second death. In mercy, God made these appointments in the future, so far as the individual is concerned. But the state of spiritual death continues while the dying-clock of the body ticks toward physical death.

Here we must distinguish the life-giving and sustaining work of the Holy Spirit from what are perceived as the laws of nature that are understood and utilized by medical science. Life is the gift of God and it is sustained in us by the Holy Spirit who makes life to abound. Any means employed to sustain life and prevent death avails only with the blessing of God and the work of His Spirit in

---

5. Charles Spurgeon. "An Awful Premonition," from *Metropolitan Tabernacle Pulpit*, vol. 10, no. 594 (London: Passmore & Alabaster, 1864), 578.

our bodies. Though God is much more powerful than any means, such as medicine, and can heal without using any means at all, one significant way God often "delays" death is through His blessing of medical science. This is a gracious means and not an end. Although certainly not as effective as modern medicine, the same could be said of medical care throughout history. In fact, when medicine has been used appropriately at any time, it lessened suffering, granted unbelievers more time to escape their state of spiritual death, and permitted believers more time to minister to others through sharing the gospel, as well as other practical acts of love, mercy, and compassion. It is crucial for Christians to understand that dying and death are not primarily medical problems, but rather to see them in the context of sin and the state of alienation sin has caused. Anything less than this may lead to idolizing medicine, physical healing, and longevity only for longevity's sake. That is not to say that it is idolatry in itself to desire life and to love many days (Ps. 34:12). The desire for longevity motivated by a God-given appreciation for the worth of His precious gift of life is something altogether different from idolizing longevity to a degree that longevity becomes more important to us than submitting to God's will.

Jesus has overcome death and dying as the Second Adam. He will eradicate both from the Christian's experience when He returns to establish everlasting healing and life. He will resurrect the dead bodies of Christians and reunite them to their living souls. Believers will live forever in the presence of Jesus and the Father and the Holy Spirit in the renewed Eden. There they will feast on the tree of life, death will be defeated, and dying will be abolished. "Blessed and holy is he that hath part in the first resurrection: on such the second death hath no power, but they shall be priests of God and of Christ, and shall reign with him a thousand years" (Rev. 20:6). Those experiencing the "first resurrection," a resurrection from spiritual death during this life, enter the community of the living church where they are living sacrifices (priests) and royal children (kings). They will not experience the "second death."

In Revelation 20, just as the second death in hellfire is the ultimate punishment (v. 14) after the first death of the body, so the first
resurrection is a gift of spiritual life before the second resurrection
of the body (vv. 12–13). A spiritual resurrection precedes the physical resurrection, as Christ taught (John 5:24–29), for believers are
united to Him who is the resurrection and life—even after they die
(John 11:25–26; Col. 3:1–4; cf. Matt. 22:23–32).[6]

---

6. Joel R. Beeke, *Revelation*, in *The Lectio Continua: Expository Commentary on
the New Testament*, ed. Joel R. Beeke and Jon D. Payne (Grand Rapids: Reformation
Heritage Books, 2016), 521–22.

Part Two

Jesus's Dying and Death

5

DYING DEVOTION
Jesus in Gethsemane (1)

Genuine devotion is inseparable from consecration and loyalty. In Christianity, to be truly devoted to God as His children is to worship God alone, to be consecrated to do His will in all things, to serve Him, and to exercise genuine zeal and piety for the triune God and His kingdom. Such devotion entails great reverence for God and earnestness in obeying Him and submitting to His will. It involves having "the single eye, Thy name to glorify."[1]

No one has ever lived so devotedly—so single-mindedly, worshipfully, and submissively—for the will and kingdom of God as Jesus. Jesus's consciousness of His unique sonship with His Father controlled all of His living and thinking. As Jesus says, "I seek not mine own will, but the will of the Father which hath sent me," and "I and my Father are one" (John 5:30; 10:30). More than thirty times in the Gospel of John, Jesus speaks of "my Father."

Jesus likewise urges His disciples to let their thoughts, worship, and lives be controlled by the conviction that God is now their Father and they are His children. He tells His disciples that they are to be examples of trusting their Father and of living devotedly to Him. He asks them why they are anxious about what they will eat or drink or about their future—their Father knows that they have need of all these things (Matt. 6:28, 31–32). Because their entire lives must be directed to glorifying their Father by obeying His will,

---

1. *The Psalter, with Doctrinal Standards, Liturgy, and Church Order* (1965; repr., Grand Rapids: Reformation Heritage Books, 2010), no. 236, stanza 2.

Jesus teaches His disciples to pray, "Our Father which art in heaven, Hallowed be thy name. Thy kingdom come. Thy will be done in earth, as it is in heaven" (Matt. 6:9–10). The child of God is to live his whole life—including his dying and death—in devoted submission to his Father.

No one serves as a better mentor in how to do this than Jesus Himself. That becomes apparent not only in what Jesus says about Himself and His ministry in relation to His Father, as we have just seen, but also in how devoted He was to His Father's will when He came face to face with death. This is particularly clear in the two greatest sites of His sufferings, Gethsemane and Calvary. His dying devotion was absolutely pure and sinless. In this chapter and the next, we will limit ourselves to considering that devotion in the Garden of Gethsemane and then, in the following chapter, we will consider His dying sufferings on the cross.

Devoted Drinker of the Cup

John 18 introduces us to the greatest day in the history of the world: the final twenty-four hours of Jesus's life prior to His crucifixion and death. How packed with action these hours are! In John 18, Jesus enters the Holy Place as our High Priest where He will tread the winepress of God's wrath. The culmination of His dying sufferings began with the agonizing events that took place in the Garden of Gethsemane.

It begins in the evening with His eating the Passover with the twelves disciples. To them He said, "With desire I have desired to eat this passover with you before I suffer" (Luke 22:15). Greater love has no man than this! Turning to John 18, we see that, after dinner, Jesus and the disciples leave Jerusalem. Christ is about to lay down His life for His disciples, including those who were just disputing about who was the greatest among them, those who would forsake Him in His darkest hours, and the one who would deny Him that night. They leave Jerusalem through the gate north of the temple, cross the Kedron Valley, and enter into "a garden" (John 18:1).

This garden was known as Gethsemane, on the lower slopes of the Mount of Olives where large olive trees grew, and where the Lord had often gone to pray. This time He went apart not only to pray but also to suffer incredible agony as well as betrayal, arrest, and captivity—"knowing all things that should come upon him" (v. 4).

Does that give you pause? Consider that Jesus went forth, knowing that His disciples would abandon Him, knowing the bitter suffering that was required to make satisfaction for His people's sins, and knowing the betrayal that Judas, His hand-picked disciple—one of the twelve—had already negotiated with the Jewish authorities. Jesus went forth, knowing that He would be whipped and beaten and spat upon, knowing that the hairs of His beard would be plucked out, and knowing that great nails would be driven through His hands and feet. Jesus went forth, knowing how full and how bitter the cup was that He must drink, down to its dregs. He must be delivered into the hands of wicked men, be crucified, and abide for three dark hours under the wrath of God in the torments of hell itself, until at last He would give Himself up to the power of death itself. Knowing all this, He went forth undaunted and strong in His determination to finish the work His Father had given Him to do in this world. What unfathomable submission and devotion to His Father's will!

Jesus went forth not as a martyr or a helpless victim, but as the willing Suffering Servant of Jehovah, as the Lion of the tribe of Judah, as the Lamb of God. Only eleven disciples entered into Gethsemane with Jesus, and only three of those were invited to go with Him still farther into the shadows and quiet of the garden. But even those three could not enter all the way into His devoted, submissive sufferings. Moving a stone's throw beyond His three best friends, Jesus fell to the earth and cried out to God, asking if there could be any alternative to drinking this bitter cup of suffering: "Father, if thou be willing, remove this cup from me: nevertheless not my will, but thine, be done" (Luke 22:42). His Father's deafening silence made the answer plain. No, the cup must be emptied, and Jesus most willingly drank from it—yes, drank it dry. There are no words

strong enough to express His suffering as He drank the Father's cup
in this garden. Mark says that He was "sore amazed" (Mark 14:33);
Luke, that He was "in an agony" (Luke 22:44); and Matthew, that
He cried out: "My soul is exceeding sorrowful, even unto death"
(Matt. 26:38). In sum, Jesus was overwhelmed, immersed, and bur-
dened down with grief. The full weight of sin—of all the sins His
people had ever or would ever commit and the hell that all those
sins deserved—together with the awful curse that His Father placed
upon their sin was pressed down upon Him until He crawled on
the ground as a worm, sweating great drops of blood as His choicest
friends slept and His greatest enemies approached to betray Him.

If the power of His Godhead had not sustained Him, Jesus
could not have endured the horrors of Gethsemane, to say nothing
of what was to follow. No one will ever comprehend the magnitude
of the sufferings of Jesus as the King-Lamb in this awesome hour at
Gethsemane. Drinking of that cup brought Him very close to the
Jordan of death—and yet there was not a word of complaint from
the lips of this devoted sufferer. What a devoted drinker He was of
the cup of His Father's wrath!

Devoted Sovereign King

John goes on in chapter 18, however, to explain for us that Jesus
was not only a devoted drinker of His Father's cup of wrath, but His
devotion included being both sovereign King (vv. 7–8) and submissive Lamb (vv. 12–13). Let's consider this King's threefold sovereignty
and this Lamb's threefold submission—both of which will make His
devotion in preparation for His death shine all the more.

After His third session of prayer, Jesus went forth to meet
Judas, officers from the chief priests, Pharisees, and a band of soldiers. During the time of Passover, hundreds of soldiers, called the
Roman "cohort" or "band," guarded the temple against revolutions
or uprisings. They were the most highly trained Roman soldiers in
the entire army. Many of the soldiers in the band came to Gethsemane well equipped; they were armed with swords and staves,

carrying torches and lamps to light their way in the night and to locate Jesus in case He tried to hide in the foliage of the olive trees. They approached the garden to surround it and tighten the noose around Jesus. No doubt they expected to find Him cowering under one of the olives trees, hiding behind its foliage like a defeated dictator cowering in a pit. Perhaps they were concerned that He and His followers would offer armed resistance. The only uncertainty was whether they had the right man. That was solved by arranging for Judas to kiss the one they were looking for. The plans were complete; the religious leaders were determined that Jesus will not escape this time.

The King's Sovereign Question

Suddenly Jesus takes charge as Gethsemane's King. He walks boldly into the moonlight and asks the sovereign question: "Whom seek ye?" (John 18:4). Judas is so intent on his devilish plans that he is blinded to Jesus's sudden display of His royal glory—and boldly kisses the Savior (Mark 14:44–45). The band of soldiers is prepared to surround the garden and lift their lamp-poles high to search for a man in hiding. But now Jesus steps boldly into the light and asks with kingly authority, "Whom seek ye?"

We are all seekers, but what or whom do we seek? Jesus, the only Savior? Then, what kind of Jesus do we seek? The multitude in the garden also seeks Jesus. They want "Jesus of Nazareth"— literally, "Jesus the Nazarene." Nazareth is considered a place of reproach; you may recall how Nathaniel asked, "Can there any good thing come out of Nazareth?" (John 1:46). Though the title *Jesus of Nazareth* can be used reverently (for example, Acts 2:22), this multitude is implying that Jesus is a false prophet and a wicked man. They want to arrest Jesus so they can ridicule, despise, and trample upon Him.

What kind of Jesus are you seeking? Millions of people today say they have received Christ, yet they give little or no evidence that they have been spiritually awakened from the dead. They do not need Jesus as Savior *and* Lord. They remain unresponsive to His

spiritual beauty and glory. Unlike Paul, they do not count everything loss for the sake of the excellency and surpassing worth of
knowing Christ Jesus as the altogether lovely Bridegroom and Lord
(Phil. 3:8).

John Piper describes this problem well:

> When these people say they "receive Christ," they do not
> receive him as *supremely valuable*. They receive him sim-
> ply as sin-forgiver (because they love being guilt-free), and
> as rescuer-from-hell (because they love being pain-free),
> and as healer (because they love being disease-free), and as
> protector (because they love being safe), and as prosperity-
> giver (because they love being wealthy), and as Creator
> (because they want a personal universe), and as Lord of
> history (because they want order and purpose); but they
> don't receive him as supremely and personally valuable for
> who he is…. They don't receive him as he really is—more
> glorious, more beautiful, more wonderful, more satisfying,
> than everything else in the universe. They don't prize *him*,
> or treasure *him*, or cherish *him*, or delight in *him*. Or to say
> it another way, they "receive Christ" in a way that requires
> no change in human nature. You don't have to be born
> again to love being guilt-free and pain-free and disease-free
> and safe and wealthy. All natural men without any spiritual
> life love these things. But to embrace Jesus as your supreme
> treasure requires a new nature. No one does this naturally.
> You must be born again (John 3:3). You must be a new cre-
> ation in Christ (2 Cor. 5:17; Gal. 6:15). You must be made
> spiritually alive (Eph. 2:1–4).[2]

The King's Sovereign Self-identification
Jesus then responds to the multitude with a second manifestation
of His kingship, declaring His sovereign self-identification. He says

---

2. John Piper, *Think: The Life of the Mind and the Love of God* (Wheaton, Ill.:
Crossway, 2010), 71.

simply, yet profoundly, "I am he" (John 18:5). *Ego eimi*—literally, "I am." As He does in other "I am" statements in the Gospel of John, it appears that here too Jesus is proclaiming His deity. In John 8:58, Jesus says, "Before Abraham was, I am." In response, the Jews took up stones to kill Him. Jesus now uses the same language that God used in naming Himself in Exodus 3 and is repeated throughout Isaiah 40–55, in identifying Himself as "I am" (Jehovah or Yahweh— "I am that I am"). Leon Morris writes, "The soldiers had come out secretly to arrest a fleeing peasant. In the gloom they find themselves confronted by a commanding figure, who so far from running away comes out to meet them and speaks to them in the very language of deity."[3]

Jesus's proclamation has such profound effects on the multitude that the people fall backward to the ground (John 18:6). What good are all the torches, lamps, swords, staves, officers, soldiers, and captains against Jesus who proclaims that He is the great "I am"—the great Jehovah, the unchangeable covenant-keeping God who was, is, and will always be what He is? Even in the state of His humiliation, one word from Jesus's lips is enough to make an entire multitude fall to the ground.

Gethsemane's King lets the confused and frightened band of soldiers get back on their feet. With royal authority, He then repeats the question: "Whom seek ye?" (John 18:7a). At this point, do you not want to cry out to the multitude: "Do you not understand that the One you are seeking to arrest is not only Jesus of Nazareth but the very Son of God? Don't you see the danger of challenging this King? Repent! Repent and bow before Him before He destroys you."

But the multitude is still totally blind. Incredibly, they repeat their first answer, "Jesus of Nazareth" (John 18:7). We should not be surprised. God is a God of second chances, but unbelievers will continue to cling to their rejection of God's Word if the Holy Spirit does not cause the scales to fall from their eyes.

---

3. Leon Morris, *The Gospel According to John* (Grand Rapids: Eerdmans, 1995), 658.

The King's Sovereign Substitution

To their second rejection of Him, Gethsemane's King not only speaks with a sovereign question and sovereign self-identification, but also with sovereign substitution. "I have told you that I am he: if therefore ye seek me, let these go their way" (John 18:8). What a staggering expression of kingly love this is! Not a single soldier dares to draw his sword against Jesus or His disciples—not even when Peter lunges at Malchus and cuts off his right ear (vv. 10–11).

The famous Baptist preacher Charles Spurgeon (1834–1892) wrote, "Those words, 'if therefore ye seek me, let these go their way,' were like coats of mail to them.... The disciples walked securely in the midst of the boisterous mob.... The words of Jesus proved to be a right royal word; it was a divine word; and men were constrained to obey it."[4]

Christ's mediatorial grace for His people is expressed in verse 9: "That the saying might be fulfilled, which he spake, Of them which thou gavest me have I lost none." Protecting His disciples was more than just kindness on Christ's part; He was fulfilling the Father's commission to save His sheep. The Father has entrusted His elect to Christ for salvation, and now Christ will walk alone to the cross, suffering and dying for them, so that not one will be lost (John 6:39; 10:28; 17:2).

Christ tells the soldiers to take Him but to let His disciples go. Those who could not watch with Him even for one hour now hear their glorious King declare that He is willing to be arrested, bound, and led away as a lamb to the slaughter so that they might go free. *He* will be scourged, but not *they. He* will be crucified, but not *they* (Isa. 53:5). Truly, there is nothing more loving than when He was willing to be bound so that they would go free. These are acts of substitutionary, royal love.

---

4. Charles Spurgeon, "The Captive Savior Freeing His People," Sermon 722 on John 18:8, 9, Nov. 25, 1866, in *Metropolitan Tabernacle Pulpit,* Vol. 12 (repr., Pasadena, Tex.: Pilgrim Publications, 1973), 650.

If Jesus Christ had fled from arrest, suffering, and death at this moment or simply destroyed His enemies, our salvation would have been impossible. So He stands His ground, saying: "Let these men go," so that even cowards like us may be caught in His eternal net of love and drawn to safety with His cords of love—and above all, so that He could willingly die for us. What a devoted, sovereign King!

Conclusion

What a comfort it is for our own dying and death as Christians to know that our Savior who died for us is also our Lord and King who has control of every detail of our life and our death! As King, He has set our circumstances for life and our boundaries for death. The fact that our dying, substitutionary Priest is also our King, assures us that we can "know that all things work together for good to them that love God" (Rom. 8:28). Not even one of the hairs of our head can fall to the ground without the will of our Sovereign King (Luke 21:18); indeed, every hair is numbered (Luke 21:18).

Dear Christian, what is the worst thing that can happen to you? That you die? Remember, if you are a Christian, what you may be prone to think is the worst thing—death, will, through the person and work of your King, actually be the best thing. For what can be better than to die in Christ in order to go to be with Him forever, sin-free in Immanuel's land?

6

DYING DEVOTION
Jesus in Gethsemane (2)

In the last chapter, we studied how Jesus in the garden of Gethsemane devotedly drank the cup of His Father's wrath despite showing Himself as the sovereign King (John 18:1–11). No sooner, however, does He manifest full authority as King in a threefold way than He also shows Himself to be a devoted, submissive Lamb in the same garden in a threefold way.

Devoted Submissive Lamb
Willingly Arrested
Christ shows us His lamb-like submissiveness in three ways; first, in His willingness to be *arrested*. John 18:12 says, "Then the band and the captain and officers of the Jews took Jesus." Jesus willingly submits to the soldiers formally arresting Him for the purpose of charging Him. He voluntarily lays down His life and no one takes it from Him (John 10:17–18)! He turns Himself over to His enemies, knowing He was signing His own death sentence for the sake of His Father and His people. The King's amazing sovereignty gives way to the Lamb's equally amazing submission.

Jesus wasn't intimidated; He knew that this was His Father's appointed hour of suffering and His death would follow. He believed the Old Testament prophecies would be fulfilled. All history had been moving toward this hour of Jesus's arrest and crucifixion. God had been at work during all the previous centuries from the creation of the world and the fall of man, down to this very night, with this hour ever before Him. His Father willed it, planned it, and worked it all out. No one can tamper with God's plan—not Judas, Caiaphas, Herod, Pilate, much less the fearful disciples. God decreed the rise and fall of nations and empires for this end. He decreed that the high priest and his cohorts should conspire to kill Jesus, that Judas should betray Him into their hands, that wicked King Herod and weak Pontius Pilate should fall in with their plans.

Jesus knew what was coming. Satan's hour had arrived, but ultimately it would be Jesus's hour. In dying, He would destroy the devil who had the power of death (Heb. 2:14). He would make the destruction of death itself an absolute certainty.

That same God is in control of your life and your dying and death also. Nothing happens because of chance. When your worst fears are realized it isn't that the Son of God has stepped away from the throne of the universe, abdicating responsibility for what is happening and abandoning you to the evil that is in the world. Rather, He is operating among the affairs of men.

Everything that happens to us is according to a plan and timetable that was fixed before the foundation of the world. No one but the Lamb of God has been found worthy to execute that plan for the salvation of His people. What happens to us in this life—including our dying and our death—is all part of the will of our Father in heaven as executed by our Savior. What a comfort for a Christian!

Willingly Bound

Second, we see Christ's submission in His willingness to be *bound*. Jesus's hands are chained like those of a murderer or criminal. The soldiers bind the hands of Jesus who would have gladly gone with them unfettered. They bind those blessed hands that healed the eyes of the blind and the lame, that blessed little children, that washed His disciples' feet and broke bread for them in the Upper Room, and that dripped with bloody sweat in prayer to the Father. Jesus offers His hands to be bound in meekness and humility.

Jesus's bound hands are symbolic of much more. Let me mention four ways this is so. First, Jesus is bound to set us free from the bands of sin. Proverbs 5:22 says that by nature we are "holden with the cords of [our] sins." By grace, Jesus became sin for us (2 Cor. 5:21). Fettered with our sins, He let Himself be arrested and be held captive to free us from the captivity of sin and Satan, and from the bondage of being prisoners of hell. Therefore, when He arose and ascended on high, He led captivity captive—bound by the cords of love—to capture His people in the net of His substitutionary gospel. By His Spirit, He is still drawing sinners with those devoted bands of love today.

Second, Jesus is bound so that His people might be bound to Him by obedience and love to serve Him all their days—even in their dying and death. When they see Him voluntarily bound for their sake, they become willing to be His servants forever. When they see Him bound for their sake, no persecution becomes too much. When they view His bonds, their afflictions and trials are sweetened and sanctified. They may even rejoice in suffering under His banner of love as did Paul and Silas, who sang in prison and counted it joy that they were reckoned worthy to suffer for Christ's sake (Acts 16:25). When the early church father Ignatius was bound and chained for confessing Christ, he regarded his bands as spiritual pearls. Do you know the joy of being bound for Christ's sake as His willing servant?

Third, Jesus is bound as the Second Adam to restore in the Garden of Gethsemane what was lost by the first Adam in the Garden of Eden. (1) The first Adam sinned in the Garden of Eden; the Second Adam bore sin in the Garden of Gethsemane. (2) The first Adam was surrounded with glory, beauty, and harmony in Eden yet refused to obey; the Second Adam was surrounded with bitterness and sorrow in Gethsemane and was obedient unto death. (3) The first Adam was tempted by Satan and fell; the Second Adam was tempted by all the forces of hell, and did not fall. (4) The first Adam's hands reached out to grasp sin; the Second Adam's hands were bound to pay for sin. (5) The first Adam was guilty and arrested by God during the cool of the day; the Second Adam was innocent and arrested by men in the middle of the night. (6) The first Adam hid himself after fleeing; the Second Adam revealed Himself

after walking into the moonlight. (7) The first Adam took fruit from
Eve's hand; the Second Adam took the cup from His Father's hand.
(8) The first Adam was conquered by the devil; the Second Adam
conquered the devil. (9) The first Adam was driven out of Eden; the
Second Adam was willingly led out of Gethsemane so that room
might be made in the heavenly garden of paradise for sinners who
trust in Him. Praise be to God—Christ regained all that was lost in
Adam, and more. In Eden, the sword was drawn and the conflict
of the ages began; in Gethsemane the sword was sheathed, and the
eternal gospel was displayed.

Finally, Jesus is bound above all by the will of the Father. He
"spared not his own Son" that His people might be spared (Rom.
8:32). His being bound is one of the ingredients of the cup that He
had to swallow in paying for the sins of His people. He was bound
to His own work which He had undertaken from eternity. He was
bound to fulfill the eternal covenant of redemption. God bound by
God—how wondrous our God of salvation is!

In the Garden of Gethsemane, Christ is the lowly Servant of
the Lord. He did not come to earth to do His own will but to do
the will of Him who sent Him. Spurgeon said, "You are clear that
he went willingly, for since a single word made the captors fall to
the ground, what could he not have done? Another word and they
would have descended into the tomb; another, and they would have
been hurled into hell.... There was no power on earth that could
possibly have bound the Lord Jesus, had he been unwilling."[1]

Willingly Led Away

Third, we see the Lamb's submission in His being *led away* (John
18:13). The Leader and Shepherd of God's people is led away as a
"lamb to the slaughter." "He was oppressed, and he was afflicted, yet
he opened not his mouth: he is brought as a lamb to the slaughter,

---

1. Spurgeon, "The Captive Savior Freeing His People," 650.

and as a sheep before her shearers is dumb, so he openeth not his mouth" (Isa. 53:7).

It is remarkable how fully this prophecy was fulfilled. Sheep that were fed in the fields of Kidron were often led through a sheep-gate to be sacrificed. This was a type of the messianic Lamb of God to come, for the Lamb of lambs is now led through that same gate to be sacrificed to die for His people. He is led from place to place like a wandering sheep so that we, who are wandering sheep, might find rest and guidance in Him.

Jesus is led a total distance of seven miles before being cruci-fied. He is led from Annas to Caiaphas to Pilate to Herod, back to Pilate and then to the cross to be crucified. What dying devo-tion belongs to this innocent Lamb who not only lets Himself be taken and bound but is willing to be taken from place to place while knowing that His end will be the cross!

How Should We Respond?

Let us ever thank the triune God for our great substitutionary Lamb, who was led away so that we might one day be led into heav-enly mansions! Have you ever seen such a devoted, complete, and willing substitute? Jesus is a perfect *seven*-mile Savior! Praise God that He was taken for criminals, bound for captives, and led away for wanderers!

In the midst of it all, He was a willing, submissive servant. We are like sponges soaked in salt water: when people press on us, we squirt out bitter words of complaint and resentment. But when Christ was crushed under malice and hatred, not one evil word came out of His mouth. His gentle devotion revealed that He was a perfect Savior and a perfect example for us.

He was *arrested* so that He can arrest us as our prophet and bring us from darkness into His marvelous light. He was *bound* so that we can be freed from the burden of sin and guilt that threat-ens to destroy us, when as priest He offered an acceptable sacrifice to God on our behalf. He was *led away* so He can govern us as our King by His Word and Spirit, leading us back to God, and preserving, guiding, and defending us in the salvation He has purchased for us.

Let us devotedly take to heart 1 Peter 2:21–25:

> For even hereunto were ye called: because Christ also suffered for us, leaving us an example, that ye should follow his steps: who did no sin, neither was guile found in his mouth: who, when he was reviled, reviled not again; when he suffered, he threatened not; but committed himself to him that judgeth righteously: who his own self bare our sins in his own body on the tree, that we, being dead to sins, should live unto righteousness: by whose stripes ye were healed. For ye were as sheep going astray; but are now returned unto the Shepherd and Bishop of your souls.

What a wonder it is that the great Deliverer delivered Himself up; the divinely appointed Judge was arrested as a common criminal; the great Liberator was bound; the great Leader was led away! Let us praise Gethsemane's Christ, the King of kings and the Lamb of God, and resolve to trust Him more fully, follow Him more obediently, and look the more expectantly for His return to take us to Himself. Let us take with us five practical ways in which Christ, as Gethsemane's King and Lamb, should impact not only our faith and life, but particularly our dying and death:

- Let us submit to the trials He imposes on us in our dying without complaint—indeed, with cheerfulness and thanksgiving—so that we may drink the cup He places in our hands rather than to plead for another.

- Let us learn to know when silence in our dying process is a more powerful testimony in the presence of evil and unbelief than any words we might say.

- Like Paul, let us cherish the privilege of being admitted to the fellowship of His sufferings through our dying and death.

- Let us honor His giving up of Himself for us with more complete surrender of ourselves to Him, so that we would be His willing servant, now and forever, in all of our daily dying.

- Let us respond to Christ's dying devotion in Gethsemane by devotedly bowing before Him, asking for grace to be willing to die in, for, with, and unto Him who was willing to die for us so that we might live forever.

7

DYING DEFEATED
Jesus Conquering Death

Jesus defeated and conquered death through His death for all those whom the Father had given Him, those who shall come to trust in Him alone for salvation. The Puritan John Owen expressed it well in the title of his magisterial volume on Christ's atonement: *The Death of Death in the Death of Christ*. To begin to comprehend this, let's go to the nadir of His sufferings in His last hours and from there to the empty tomb, the final judgment, and to heaven itself.

The Profundity of Christ's Dying Sufferings
It is noon on Good Friday, and Jesus has been on the cross for three pain-filled hours. Suddenly darkness falls on Calvary and over all the land. By a miraculous act of Almighty God, midday becomes midnight. This supernatural darkness is a symbol of God's judgment on sin. The physical darkness signals a deeper and more fearsome darkness. It declares, as we have seen, that "the wages of sin is death" (Rom. 6:23).

The great High Priest enters Golgotha's holy of holies without His friends or His enemies. The Son of God is alone on the cross for three final hours, enduring what defies our imagination. Experiencing the full brunt of His Father's wrath, Jesus cannot stay silent. He cries out: "My God, my God, why hast thou forsaken me?" (Matt. 27:46).

This word from the cross represents the nadir, the lowest point, of Jesus's sufferings. Here Jesus descends into the essence of hell, the most extreme suffering ever experienced in human history. It is a time so compacted, yet so infinite, and so horrendous as to be incomprehensible and seemingly unsustainable.

What does this cry of dereliction actually mean? Before we stammer a little about its meaning, let's remind ourselves of what it does not mean in four succinct points: (1) Jesus's cry of dereliction does not in any way diminish His deity. Jesus does not cease being God before, during, or after this. (2) Jesus's cry does not divide His human nature from His divine person or somehow destroy the Trinity. (3) Jesus's cry does not detach Him from the Holy Spirit. The Son lacks the comforts of the Spirit, but He does not lose the holiness of the Spirit. And finally, (4) Jesus's cry does not cause Him to disavow His mission. Both the Father and Son knew from all eternity that Jesus would become the Lamb of God who would suffer and die to take away the sin of the world (Acts 15:18). It is unthinkable that the Son of God might question what is happening or be perplexed about His mission when His Father's loving presence departs.

So what does this cry mean? (1) Jesus is expressing the agony of *unanswered supplication* (Ps. 22:1–2). Think of it—the Father not answering that Son who could say the Father always hears Him (John 11:42)! Unanswered, Jesus feels profoundly forgotten of God, which brings Him unspeakable pain in His soul. (2) Jesus is also expressing the agony of *unbearable stress*. It is the kind of "groaning" or "roaring" mentioned in Psalm 22:1: the groan and roar of desperate agony without rebellion. It is the awful, agonizing cry uttered when the undiluted wrath of God overwhelms the soul. It is heart-piercing, heaven-piercing, and hell-piercing. (3) Further, Jesus is expressing the agony of *unmitigated sin*. All the sins of the elect, and the hell that they eternally deserve are laid upon Him as a compressed and seemingly unbearable weight. (4) Finally, Jesus is expressing the agony of *unassisted solitariness*. In His hour of greatest need comes a pain unlike anything Christ has ever experienced: His Father's abandonment. When Jesus most needs encouragement, no voice cries from heaven, "This is my beloved Son" (Matt. 3:17). No angel is sent to strengthen Him; no "Well done, good and faithful servant" (Matt. 25:23) resounds in His ears. The women who supported Him are silent. The disciples, cowardly and terrified, have fled. Feeling disowned by all, hanging between heaven and earth and hell, without even the sun of nature to shine upon Him, Jesus endures the way of suffering alone, deserted, and forsaken in utter darkness.

Every detail of this horrific abandonment declares the heinous character of our sins. Oh the profundity of Christ's sufferings on behalf of sin! As Luther said, after meditating on Jesus's cry of dereliction for hours: "God forsaken of God! Who can comprehend it?"

The Purpose behind Christ's Dying Sufferings

Why would God bruise His own Son (Isa. 53:10)? The Father is not capricious, malicious, or being merely didactic. The real purpose is *penal*; it is the just punishment for the sin of Christ's people. Paul could not be plainer: "For he hath made him to be sin for us, who knew no sin; that we might be made the righteousness of God in him" (2 Cor. 5:21).

Christ was made sin *"for* us," dear believers. Among all the mysteries of salvation, this little word *for* exceeds all. This small word illuminates our darkness and unites Jesus Christ with sinners. Christ was acting on our behalf and for our benefit as our representative.

With Jesus as our substitute, God's justice is satisfied and God can justify those of us who believe in Jesus alone for salvation (Rom. 3:26). Christ's penal suffering, therefore, is vicarious—He suffered on our behalf. He did not simply share our forsakenness, but He saved us from it. He endured it *for* us, not *with* us. Let this truth sink deeply into your soul: You are immune to condemnation (Rom. 8:1) and to God's *anathema* (Gal. 3:13) because Christ bore it for you in that outer darkness. Golgotha secured our immunity, not mere sympathy. The Scottish theologian John "Rabbi" Duncan (1796–1870) put it so well: "Do you know what it was—dying on the cross, forsaken by His Father—do you know what it was?… It was damnation—and damnation taken lovingly."[1]

This explains the hours of darkness and the roar of dereliction. God's people experience just a taste of this when, in their conversion, they are brought by the Holy Spirit before the Judge of heaven and earth, only to experience that they are not consumed for Christ's sake. They come out of darkness, confessing, "Because Immanuel has descended into the lowest hell for us, God is with us in the darkness, under the darkness, through the darkness—and we are not consumed!"

The Love Pervading Christ's Dying Sufferings

How stupendous is the *love of Christ!* His love is so vividly displayed in His cry, "My God, my God, why hast thou forsaken me?" It was the cry of the incarnate God whose soul was sinking ever deeper into the bottomless pit of divine wrath.

How stupendous is the *love of the Father!* The Father gives His only Son (John 3:16), His bosom Friend from eternity; He took the best He had and offered Him for the worst He could find—sinners like us. He held nothing in reserve but extravagantly loved sinners who were at enmity with Him.

How stupendous is the *love of the Spirit!* He works patiently yet irresistibly in the hearts of sinners, applying to us the cross's wonderful truth and salvation. He convinces us that all our sufferings, including feeling forsaken, are merely the fruit of walking in Jesus's shadow. Our hearts so overflow with love that we respond, "We love him, because he first loved us" (1 John 4:19).

The Victorious Completion of Christ's Dying Sufferings

Having come through this incredible, agonizing suffering of soul and body, Jesus then cries out in the sixth word He spoke from the

---

1. A. Moody Stuart, *Recollections of the Late John Duncan* (Edinburgh: Edmonston and Douglas, 1872), 105.

cross, "*Tetelestai!*"—just one word, but in English, "It is finished" (John 19:30). Never has so much content ever been poured into one word in human history. The Greeks boasted that they could convey an ocean of matter in a drop of language, but surely here Jesus has outdone them all.

What did Jesus "finish?" With respect to *His Father*, (1) He finished the work given to Him as the Servant of the Father, a work that needed to be accomplished in our human flesh. He finished this work in perfect agreement with the eternal counsel of peace, fulfilling the will of His Father for the glorification of the triune God's holy attributes so that God can be just and the justifier of him who believes in Jesus alone for salvation. (2) Further, He fulfilled all the prophecies, types, shadows, and promises of the Old Testament economy with respect to His own state of humiliation as the suffering Messiah. (3) He fulfilled all of the Old Testament ceremonial laws and typical sacrifices, so that His Father as judge could immediately tear the veil of the temple from top to bottom (Mark 15:37–39). That tearing signified the end of the Aaronic priesthood and the entire system of ceremonial laws that were to find their fulfillment in the completed work of salvation in the coming Messiah.

With respect to *Himself,* this cry meant that (1) Jesus finished His sufferings as the substitute for His people and gave His own life as a ransom price for them. As the Dutch Lord's Supper form says so beautifully: He "confirmed with his death and shedding of his blood, the new and eternal testament, that covenant of grace and reconciliation, when he said: 'It is finished.'"[2] With this cry, He could now commend His spirit to His Father and lay down His life. (2) With this loud cry Jesus not only went out to meet death, to pass through death, to conquer death, but also to destroy death— not only for Himself, but for all those the Father had given to Him to save. It was a loud, victorious cry because it contained the triumphant note of victory. It was not the weak, defeated cry of a dying

---

2. "Doctrinal Standards, Liturgy, and Church Order," in *The Psalter,* 2:137.

man who became a victim of martyrdom; it was not the gasp of a worn-out life, but it was the cry of victory, of triumph, of completion, by the Conqueror of all ages in the full flush of victory over every enemy.

And with respect to those of us who are *true believers*, He finished the battle against all our enemies as complete Victor. He conquered sin as the sinless one to the very end of His life. He finished bearing the curse of sin, so that sin will not have dominion over us (Rom. 6:14). He conquered Satan, destroying him who had the power over death, through His own death (Heb. 2:14–15). He destroyed death, sanctified the grave, and conquered hell for us, robbing them all of their power, taking their keys away from them as Victor (Rev. 1:18). He finished the work of redemption for us, so that through His passive obedience in paying for our sins and His active obedience in fulfilling the law for us, He has merited eternal life. Therefore, He can apply everything that we need to be saved through His double obedience to those who trust Him alone for their salvation.

What a comfort for sin-weary souls that there is nothing left for us to accomplish because Jesus has done everything! We are justified freely by His grace unto salvation through His righteousness (Rom. 3:24). He has finished the work—*tetelestai!*

The Voluntary Surrender of Christ's Dying Sufferings

Finally, after His loud, victorious cry, anticipating the defeat of death, Jesus "bowed his head, and gave up the ghost" (John 19:30b). In other words, He gave His life voluntarily. When we die, we first die and then our head bows, but with Jesus it was the other way around. This underscores that even in all His pain His life was not taken from Him, but He gave it up voluntarily (John 10:18). That very fact contributes to His victory over death. Death did not defeat Him; He defeated death. In His death, He destroyed death forever for His people, so that now our death is but a passageway into eternal life.

The Glorious Vindication of Christ's Dying Sufferings

All of Jesus's defeating and destroying of death is gloriously under-
scored for us when He rose from the grave early on the first day of
the week. Christ's resurrection is the "Amen" of the Father upon all
the sufferings of Christ; it ratifies Paul's confession: "Death is swal-
lowed up in victory. O death, where is thy sting? O grave, where is
thy victory?" (1 Cor. 15:54–55).

Christ's death and resurrection are of one piece; they are
inseparable components of our salvation. They are, as Luther put
it, the two hinges on which the door of salvation swings open for
us. They bring together the end of Christ's state of humiliation and
the beginning of His state of exaltation. Jesus's cross and His crown;
the dying Lamb and the living conqueror; the one who merits and
applies our salvation are intimately connected in our salvation; we
cannot do without either one. We need Christ as much for what
He was on the cross as for what He is as the resurrected Lord—
and vice versa. Without a dying, humiliated Jesus, there would be
no atonement—no way for us to die in peace; without the living,
exalted Jesus, there would be no application of His salvation by His
Spirit—no way for us to live in peace.

Thank God that His Son has destroyed death through His cross
and His resurrection. One day, He will destroy death utterly and
forever when He ushers us into the realm of glory where there
will be no more death. There, in heaven, all evil and dying will be
walled out and all good and true life will be walled in—forever! *Soli
Deo gloria!*

8

DYING DESTROYED
No More Death

"For we have not an high priest which cannot be touched with the feeling of our infirmities," says the writer of Hebrews, but one who, "was in all points tempted like as we are, yet without sin" (4:15)— "Jesus the Son of God" (v. 14). Although this passage focuses on the fact that Jesus did not yield to temptation, it also points to a more fundamental truth about Him—He was born a sinless human being. As Paul reminds us, He "knew no sin" (2 Cor. 5:21). In fact, the Greek word translated "without" in the passage from Hebrews may also be translated "apart from." Using the word in this way carries the meaning of being in a state of separation from sin.

In relation to dying and death, this biblical truth has profound implications. Since Jesus was sinless, He was *not* "conceived in sin" (Ps. 51:5). Therefore, He was not born as one alienated from God (i.e. spiritually dead). Aging for Him was *not* a process of dying ending in physical death. Jesus did not suffer from diseases caused by faulty genes or cells; and in His human nature, He had life-giving spiritual communion with God the Father and God the Holy Spirit in every thought, word, and deed from Mary's womb until His exaltation at the Father's right hand. "In him was life, and the life was the light of men" (John 1:4)—in totality. Even during those heart-wrenching hours on the cross, the Second Adam still yearned in body and soul for communion with His heavenly Father, but for the purposes of redemption, He experienced the "dereliction" of being forsaken by God for a time (Ps. 22:1; Matt. 27:46). The inherited and inborn properties and tendencies of original sin were never a part

of Jesus's personal experience. By grace, all of our sinfulness, all our
sins, and all of the consequences of sin—including disease, decay,
dying, death, and eternal condemnation—were a burden that He
willingly took upon Himself and bore for our sake as our Mediator
and Redeemer. By "sending his own Son in the likeness of sinful
flesh, and for sin, [God] condemned sin in the flesh" (Rom. 8:3).

God Made Jesus to Be without Sin

Through the operation of the Holy Spirit, the eternal purpose of the
Father came to fruition, as the Son of God was made flesh in the
womb of a virgin named Mary. Theologian Philip Hughes explains:

> It was by means of the virgin birth that the Son of God
> took our human nature to himself.... The incarnation...
> relates back to and interprets the original unique act of
> creation...which had been dragged down by the fall of
> the first Adam.... It was necessary for Jesus Christ, the
> last Adam, to enter the world like the first Adam, inno-
> cent, God-centered, unstained by sin, and unburdened by
> guilt.... It was the birth of Jesus from a virgin mother, our
> fellow human being, that preserved the vital connectedness
> with our human nature.[1]

In Christ's holy conception and birth, at one and the same time,
Mary's child was bone of her bones and flesh of her flesh, that is,
truly human, but also "holy, harmless, undefiled, separate from
sinners" (Heb. 7:26). Christ was born into this world in a state of
innocence and righteousness, just as Adam had been created in the
state of original righteousness. Truly human and also perfectly righteous, the incarnate Son of God was all that He needed to be in
order to make full satisfaction to the justice of God for our sins, and
deliver us from the power of Satan, death, and hell.

---

1. Philip Edgcumbe Hughes, *The True Image: The Origin and Destiny of Man in Christ* (Grand Rapids: Eerdmans, 1989), 216–17.

God Made Jesus to Be Sin

Holy Scripture is clear: the incarnation of the Son of God, His life of redemptive suffering, including His death on the cross, and His resurrection and ascension, were all the outworking of God's eternal plan for our salvation. The human agents involved were unwitting instruments of a sovereign God. Peter asserts this view of events in his sermon on the day of Pentecost, when he confronts the "men of Israel," saying, "Him, being delivered by the determinate counsel and foreknowledge of God, ye have taken, and by wicked hands have crucified and slain" (Acts 2:23). Later, it was professed in the prayers of the infant church: "For of a truth against thy holy child Jesus, whom thou hast anointed, both Herod, and Pontius Pilate, with the Gentiles, and the people of Israel, were gathered together, For to do whatsoever thy hand and thy counsel determined before to be done." (Acts 4:27–28). It was on a Roman cross around AD 35, outside the walls of Jerusalem, sometime between 9:00 a.m. (Mark 15:25) until shortly after 3:00 p.m., the incarnate Son of God was made sin for us. During the three hours of darkness, Jesus descended into a hell of suffering, experiencing the horror of separation and alienation from His God and Father in heaven. He experienced the devastating power of death at work in His mortal body and, when the darkness was ended, He surrendered Himself to the power of death.

These hours on the cross were of eternal worth, which is why Matthew conflates several events with historic, cosmic, theological, and future significance. The death of the incarnate Son of God registered in the realm of nature, producing a number of extraordinary effects, both natural and supernatural, as Matthew reports: "Jesus, when he had cried again with a loud voice, yielded up the ghost. And, behold, the veil of the temple was rent in twain from the top to the bottom; and the earth did quake, and the rocks rent; and the graves were opened; and many bodies of the saints which slept arose, and came out of the graves after his resurrection, and went into the holy city, and appeared unto many" (Matt. 27:50–53).

Matthew is not merely recounting a series of historical events; but he is also describing the meaning of the Second Adam's death. There is more to these effects than the casual reader may discern. As D. A. Carson notes in his commentary on Matthew:

> The tearing of the veil and the opening of the tombs together symbolize the first of twin foci in Jesus' death and resurrection. On the one hand, Jesus' sacrificial death blots out sin, defeats the powers of evil and death, and opens up access to God. On the other, Jesus' victorious resurrection and vindication promise the final resurrection of those who die in him…. Jesus' work on the cross is tied to his impending resurrection; together they open up the new age and promise of eschatological life.[2]

The earthquake, the rending of the curtain in the temple to open a way of access into the presence of God, the tombs giving up the bodies of the righteous dead, the resurrection or reunion of their souls and bodies and their appearances in Jerusalem, all point to the powerful historic, present, and future transformation and renewal of all things including human beings accomplished by Christ's death and resurrection (cf. Rom. 8:18–23; Rev. 21, 22).

In the three hours of darkness, Jesus was "forsaken" or deprived of communion with His Father and He began to experience "the suffering of death" so that "he by the grace of God should taste death for every man" (Heb. 2:9). Some of the Reformed Confessions speak of Christ descending into hell while hanging on the cross. Jesus was "counted with them that go down into the pit…as a man that hath no strength: Free among the dead, like the slain that lie in the grave," like those whom His Father refuses to remember (Ps. 88:4–5). Outside the walls of Jerusalem, in the place of public execution, overcast by the smoke of the Hinnom Valley, under a blackened sky with the light of the sun blotted out, beaten, bloodied, and pierced

---

2. Don A. Carson, *Matthew*, in *The Expositor's Bible Commentary*, ed. Frank E. Gaebelein (Grand Rapids: Zondervan, 1984), 581–82.

with nails, Jesus hung on a Roman cross rejected by heaven and earth as a dying substitute for sinners, surrounded by His mocking, jeering, and teeth-gnashing dead-in-spirit fellow men—this was nothing less than hell on earth.[3]

The blessings of the Father were withdrawn, and Jesus Christ experienced the punishment of the triune Creator as a guilty man for the sin of all those whom the Father had given Him. For those three hours of eternal merit, Jesus endured the essence of hell, which is the state of perpetual absence from the mercy of God and a continual experience of dying underneath His just wrath for sin. It was an ongoing state of spiritual death, lacking God's common graces for physical, psychological, and spiritual comfort. Jesus Christ endured spiritual death on the cross until He satisfied the just demands of the triune Creator, and when it was over He declared: "It is finished: and he bowed his head, and gave up the ghost" (John 19:30).

After Jesus died, His righteous soul was taken to "paradise" (Luke 23:43), and Joseph of Arimathea secured His lifeless body and laid it in his tomb (vv. 50–53), but in three days the human soul of Jesus was reunited with His body and He rose to newness of life in victory over physical death and dying (24:1–6). "Christ being raised from the dead dieth no more; death hath no more dominion over him. For in that he died, he died unto sin once: but in that he liveth, he liveth unto God" (Rom. 6:9–10).

The Son of God left His glorious throne in heaven to become the sinless Jesus of Nazareth. For thirty-three years He lived a life of perfect communion with His Father, but He always had an eye on the death sentence for sin He was appointed to serve for others.

---

3. The phrase in the Apostles' Creed, "he descended into hell," has been interpreted as Jesus going to hell to do battle with Satan after He died, or some other variation on this theme (cf. Eph. 4:8–10; 1 Pet. 3:18–20). This is not the place to explore the merits of this doctrine, but what is abundantly clear from Scripture is that Jesus endured the punishment for sin in its entirety on the cross. When this was done, he declared "it is finished" and died (John 19:30).

"Tasting death" for hell-worthy sinners, He experienced the dying of the body. As the sin-bearer, He experienced the essence of hell, or the separation of the soul from God and finally, He willingly laid down His life, embracing and conquering death, and commending His soul to God. Jesus Christ destroyed dying by His own death, and buried sin, guilt, and death in Joseph of Arimathea's tomb. Then He rose again, so that by faith "we might be made the righteousness of God in him" (2 Cor. 5:21) and possess a sure hope that we too will overcome dying and death just like He did through the resurrection of our bodies on the last day.

In the chapters to come, we will explore contemporary issues relating to dying and death and how to approach them with a firm faith and well-founded hope empowered by love in our great High Priest, who has opened the way into the healing and life-giving presence of the triune Creator. We will consider a variety of topics, such as disobeying biblical principles in an attempt to prolong physical life at all costs and ending one's own life by committing suicide, as well as being ill prepared to face death and dying. Most importantly, we will reflect on a faithful, hopeful, and loving journey with brothers and sisters as they draw near to the gates of eternity. As they experience the dying of their bodies we will consider how they are supported by the physical and spiritual graces God provides and how we can administer the medicine of compassion, wisdom, and strength to each other in the context of Christ's hospital, the church.

Part Three

Contemporary Issues

9

DYING DESPERATELY
Pursuing Futile Treatment

The Westminster Shorter Catechism's Question 68 teaches that the sixth commandment "requireth all lawful endeavours to preserve our own life," and by the grace of God, we have many "lawful" ways to do that today. The Westminster divines had in mind, however, not just the laws of man, but also the law of God. Something may be lawful according to the laws of man, but not according to the law of God. Thus, the Catechism speaks of "all *lawful* endeavours," not "all *possible* endeavours." Today, we have defibrillators to restart stalled hearts, ventilators to sustain breathing, dialysis machines to filter blood, and a seemingly limitless arsenal of pharmaceutical agents for treating almost every condition. Modern western medicine aside, we also have a plethora of "alternative medicine" options as well. In a day when William Harvey offered the first comprehensive explanation of the human circulatory system (1628), it was not possible for the Westminster divines to fully understand what "all lawful endeavours to preserve our own life" would become in the twenty-first century. There is an understandably human, but still sinful, impulse on the part of many to prolong life and escape death by any means available, including futile procedures, debilitating treatments, experimental cures, and even resorting to medical quackery, mind cures, and faith healing, in a desperate bid for a miracle.

When I (Bogosh) first started writing about the intersection of modern medicine and a biblical worldview for medical science in 2009, I concentrated on hope. Much of what I encountered as both a nurse and a pastor was unrealistic optimism focused on curing a disease, not only among unbelievers, but among believers as well. Fueled by words of "hope for a cure" offered to them by physicians of various stripes, these individuals in the final stages of dying often cast off realism and put on the blinders of denial in an attempt to escape death at all costs. Sometimes a few more weeks were added to the calendar, but the patient ultimately died, usually with misery multiplied for those they loved and for themselves.

The late Dr. Sherwin B. Nuland, a practicing physician for more than a half-century and author of the popular book, *How We Die*, offered these telling observations about well-meaning healthcare professionals, the "hope for a cure" they offer, and modern man's eagerness to embrace these hopes in order to avoid death:

> Too often, physicians misunderstand the ingredients of hope, thinking it only refers to cure.... Sometimes it is really to maintain his own hope that the doctor deludes himself into a course of action whose odds of success seem too small to justify embarking on it. Rather than seeking ways to help his patient face the reality that life must soon come to an end, he indulges a very sick person and himself in a form of medical "doing something" to deny the hovering presence of death. This is one of the ways in which his profession manifests the entire society's current refusal to admit the existence of death's power, and perhaps even death itself.[1]

Dr. Nuland was not a Christian by profession, but seems, nonetheless, to have come to clear and well-considered views of dying and death. He had more to say: "We have somehow been so taken up with the wonders of modern science that our society puts the emphasis in the wrong place.... In ages past, the hour of death was...seen as a time of spiritual sanctity, and of a last communion with those left behind.... This last communion was not only the

---

1. Sherwin B. Nuland, *How We Die: Reflections on Life's Final Chapter* (New York: Random House, 1995), 223–24.

focus of the sense that a good death was being granted them but of the hope they saw in the existence of God and an afterlife."[2] These are some very insightful words from an unbelieving but sincere physician, who, after decades of attempting to eradicate disease, admits defeat and encourages people not to place their ultimate hope in modern medicine.

For many Christians, doing the will of God has come to mean the pursuit of healing or medical treatment to prolong life at all costs. While a lot of wisdom is needed to decide when to receive or forgo medical treatment, God does not require us to use all possible measures at our disposal to slow the process of dying and postpone death. Our major questions should not be about living or dying, but about faithfulness while we are breathing here and now, because "whether we live, we live unto the Lord; and whether we die, we die unto the Lord." Paul enlarges helpfully on this thought in Romans 14:7–9: "For none of us liveth to himself, and no man dieth to himself. For whether we live, we live unto the Lord; and whether we die, we die unto the Lord: whether we live therefore, or die, we are the Lord's. For to this end Christ both died, and rose, and revived, that he might be Lord both of the dead and living."

Fearing Death

We might as well face it: the reason why some Christians pursue medical treatment beyond the point of reason and sense is that they fear death. In part, this fear is the outworking of a God-given instinct for life. We were created to live, not to die. But this fear can also be rooted in a lingering sense of the guilt of sin. We know that we are sinners and deserve nothing but God's wrath and curse and that death is the wages of sin (Rom. 6:23). Death presents itself as a scorpion with a deadly sting in his tail, which he claims to have the right to use on all who have sinned against God. Satan is thus able to use the fear of death as a whip to drive us onward in a desperate

---

2. Nuland, *How We Die*, 256.

bid to escape our inevitable doom. He is pleased to remind us of the righteous sentence of God's law: "The soul that sinneth, it shall die" (Ezek. 18:20).

This fear, then, can expose a lack of faith in God's promises to us in Christ. We are assailed with doubts: How can God be just, and be the justifier of the ungodly? Does the blood of Christ truly wash away all sin? Are my sins forgiven? Is there no condemnation awaiting me in the judgment to come? Though "the last enemy that shall be destroyed is death" (1 Cor. 15:26), it is still possible for Christians to persevere in faith and overcome this fear, because Jesus removed death's sting (v. 56; cf. Rom. 5:12–21), depriving death of its power to hurt us, and one day will destroy death finally and forever. "Fear not," said our glorious and victorious Physician, "I am he that liveth, and was dead; and, behold, I am alive for evermore, Amen; and have the keys of hell and of death" (Rev. 1:17–18).

Christ's Lack of Fear

Any treatment of Christ's lack of fear needs to take into account Gethsemane, where Christ clearly feared the cross. Doubtlessly, we would say that is because He understood that He would undergo wrath, not merely crucifixion. This is what undermines any accusation that Socrates faced death with an equanimity that Christ did not display. Socrates was not dying the death that Christ faced. Furthermore, Christ met this entirely rational fear with steadfastness. The crisis passed and He moved forward resolutely, despising the shame. Love for His Father and His plan of redemption along with love for His people, His treasure and portion, gave Him strength to overcome His fear and endure the cross.[3]

Thus, Christ did not die as a victim or martyr as we noted earlier. What marks both victims and martyrs is that they are passive. Suffering and death are imposed on them by powers beyond their control. This was not so with our Christ. He set His face towards

---

3. For more detail on Christ's sufferings in Gethsemane, see chapters 5 and 6.

Jerusalem. He refused rescue by legions of loyal angels. In coming into Jerusalem, He acted in ways that would declare that He was God's messianic King, notwithstanding the opposition He knew it would generate. Furthermore, He refused to do anything that would have persuaded an all-too-willing Pilate to free Him. All of this He did with full purpose of mind and heart. His life was not taken from Him, as it is with victims and martyrs. It was given by Him freely and voluntarily.

Better Options

The best place for the Christian, when he or she is facing death and dying, is not at a doctor's office or in a hospital, but at home and in the context of the church when strength permits. This does not mean Christians should not seek medical treatment, but one needs to think carefully about his medical care in the context of a biblical worldview. Like most people in the secularized West, some Christians decide to pursue aggressive medical treatment in an attempt to prolong their lives. At times God may wonderfully bless such a decision and life may be graciously prolonged, but at other times such a choice ends up isolating them from the means of grace dispensed in the services of the church. They trade the communion of the saints, the preaching of the Word, the administration of the sacraments, and the singing of praise, for a few more weeks or months of life sustained by what is often the hollow optimism of oncologists and a futile course of chemotherapy.

There are other options for treatment, if we have eyes to see them. Along with the rise of modern medicine during the twentieth century, a specialized type of medical care referred to as palliative or hospice care developed. Although not new to humankind, this type of compassionate treatment does not focus on treating the symptoms of the disease, but addresses the physical, spiritual, psychological, and social grief caused by it. One of the goals of palliative care is to keep people out of doctors' offices and hospitals. For the Christian, that means being present at home with loved ones and, while it is possible, in church with the saints feasting on the means of grace. If believers chose this kind of care, they would have the help and comfort of the Word of God and the fellowship of the church as they make their way out of this world and into the next.

The best way to be kept from dying desperately is not only to learn how to die peaceably at home and in the context of the church, surrounded by loving family members and the communion of the saints, but also, as we will see in more detail in the next chapter, to be prepared for death internally by living in Christ and for God's glory as a fruit of His Spirit's work of salvation in you. There is no better way to live, and no better way to die, for when Christ is welcome in your life you may also welcome death!

10

DYING DELIBERATELY
Wise Preparation for Death

One morning someone asked Martin Luther what he would do that day if he knew he would die that evening. He replied, rather strangely, that he would go out and plant an apple tree. The point he was making was that he was so ready to die every day due to his relationship in Christ and his living a "daily dying lifestyle" with regard to Christ's own righteousness, that there would be nothing special for him to do. John Calvin also said some remarkable things about being prepared for death:

> Although we must still meet death, let us nevertheless be calm and serene in living and dying, when we have Christ going before us. If anyone cannot set his mind at rest by disregarding death, that man should know that he has not yet gone far enough in the faith of Christ.... If we remember that by death we are called back from exile to home, to our heavenly fatherland, shall we then not be filled with comfort?
>
> We may positively state that nobody has made any progress in the school of Christ, unless he cheerfully looks forward toward the day of his death, and towards the day of the final resurrection.[1]

---

1. Blanchard, *Complete Gathered Gold*, 131.

How can we as true Christians wisely prepare ourselves for death so that we actually look forward to it while living in the midst of a world that is rampant with materialism and stuff?

Westminster Directory on Preparing for Sickness and Death

An often underappreciated, but helpful, section in the *Westminster Directory for the Publick Worship of God* (1645) is entitled, "Concerning Visitation of the Sick." I (Christopher Bogosh) wrote, *The Puritans on How to Care for the Sick and Dying: A Contemporary Guide for Pastors and Counselors*, as an exposition of this important document, tying it into the Confession of Faith and the Catechisms. "Concerning Visitation of the Sick" is full of timeless pastoral advice to help one care for the sick and dying. The Westminster divines direct that,

> The minister is to admonish his congregation in times of health in order to prepare them for sickness and death. The goal of this admonishment is to have those committed to his care speak frequently to him about the state of their souls, and in times of sickness, they are to desire his timely and appropriate advice before their strength and under-standing fail them because of sickness.[2]

Note first that the divines instruct us to admonish those in good health to prepare for death; second, how to comfort sick and dying believers with the Word of God, wise counsel, and prayer; and third, how, "with all tenderness and love," to confront those who are dying without an intelligent, well-grounded faith in Christ: "If the sick person shall declare any scruple, doubt, or temptation that are upon him, instructions and resolutions shall be given to satisfy and settle him.... It may also be useful to show him that death hath in it no spiritual evil to be feared by those that are in

---

2. Christopher W. Bogosh, "Concerning Visitation of the Sick: Updated," *The Puritans on How to Care for the Sick and Dying: A Contemporary Guide for Pastors and Counselors* (Yulee, Fla.: Good Samaritan Books, 2011), 97.

Christ, because sin, the sting of death, is taken away by Christ...that neither life nor death shall be able to separate us from God's love in Christ, in whom such are sure, though now they must be laid in the dust, to obtain a joyful and glorious resurrection to eternal life."[3] Such a Bible-based, Christ-centered perspective on sickness, death, and dying will surely go far to counter the desperate bid to prolong life and postpone death that leads so many into a very painful and miserable experience of dying as they go from one futile course of treatment to another.

Preparing for death involves entrusting ourselves to Christ spiritually, so that our lives are "hid with Christ in God" (Col. 3:3), by means of Christ's life, death, resurrection, and ascension. Preparing for death involves laying up for ourselves treasures in heaven (Matt. 6:20) while bearing fruit for Christ on earth, living evangelistic and missional lives, always aiming for God's glory and the genuine well-being of our neighbor. Preparing for death involves meditating on death biblically like the psalmists do in Psalms 39 and 90, as well as grieving over death properly—in measure rather than inordinately (1 Thess. 4:13). Preparing for death involves honoring the dead properly, attending funerals of friends and loved ones, speaking soberly yet hopefully about believers in the face of death, insisting on God-centered funerals, and honoring the body with a proper burial.[4]

The Westminster Directory says little about particulars beyond exhorting the sick and dying to put their houses in order and to take care for the payment of their debts. The biblical and theological context in which it labors to place dying and death implies most of what really needs to be said to assist believers in making decisions about medical care.

While the divines stressed the major issues concerning preparing for death, in today's world helpful and practical instructions

---

3. "Concerning Visitation of the Sick," p. 91.

4. For this paragraph, we are dependent on a helpful article by William Boekestein, "We're All Going to Die," *Outlook* 36 (Feb. 2017): 12–16.

from a more mundane perspective would include paying off debts, writing a will, organizing a funeral, and preparing medical directives. It is wise to assist our loved ones in preparing for our own death. Hence, we should engage in deliberate actions to prevent us from acting in unbiblical ways and from being an unnecessary burden to others (cf. 2 Thess. 3:8).

Fundamental Values

In our day of specialists and individualism, ministers and elders are often left outside the loop of a church member's medical decisions and end-of-life planning. A Christian visits a doctor, lawyer, financial advisor, or funeral director and makes important decisions that may impact the spiritual and material well-being of the church as a whole, but the pastor finds out after the fact—often couched in a member's request for prayer to bless the choices already made! This should not be the case, but often it is. It cuts across the grain of what it means to be a member of the body of Christ.

> And he ["he who ascended," v. 10, i.e., the risen Christ] gave...some, pastors and teachers; for the perfecting of the saints, for the work of the ministry, for the edifying of the body of Christ: till we all come in the unity of the faith, and of the knowledge of the Son of God, unto a perfect man, unto the measure of the stature of the fulness of Christ: that we henceforth be no more children, tossed to and fro, and carried about with every wind of doctrine, by the sleight of men, and cunning craftiness, whereby they lie in wait to deceive. (Eph. 4:11–14)

Ministers and ruling elders are "shepherds" (i.e., pastors), who nurture, protect, and guide, as well as being "teachers," who advise and instruct in order to equip, to build up, and to mature the entire congregation in Christ. Their calling does not stop there; they are also called upon to defend individuals in the church from the inadvertent acceptance of secular wisdom, anti-Christian strategies, and satanic deceptions that will infect the body of Christ. While most pastors do not possess the specialized training, knowledge, and experience of a doctor, lawyer, or some other professional, they *should* be equipped with the insight, guidance, and experience necessary to help church members make biblically-informed medical, legal, financial, and other end-of-life decisions.

Every faithful pastor believes, preaches, and strives to live out Jesus's teaching: "If any man will come after me, let him deny himself, and take up his cross, and follow me. For whosoever will save his life shall lose it: and whosoever will lose his life for my sake shall find it" (Matt. 16:24–25). These same pastors are also zealous to apply Paul's personal testimony to themselves and to others: "I am crucified with Christ: nevertheless I live; yet not I, but Christ liveth in me: and the life which I now live in the flesh I live by the faith of the Son of God, who loved me, and gave himself for me," and "For to me to live is Christ, and to die is gain" (Gal. 2:20; Phil. 1:21). Self-denial, bearing one's own crosses or burdens, following and losing one's own life for Christ, being crucified with Christ, no longer living a self-serving life but Christ's self-giving life, and living this present life by faith and in gratitude to "the Son of God, who loved me, and gave himself for me"—this is to be the heartfelt experience of every Christian. These are the fundamental values every Bible-believing pastor embraces and they are the same principles that need to undergird and inform every decision and plan a Christian makes.

Practical Guidelines

While it is not possible in this book to provide a list of comprehensive suggestions for medical care and end-of-life planning, some helpful resources to go to are *Compassionate Jesus: Rethinking the Christian's Approach to Modern Medicine*; *The Golden Years: Healthy Aging and the Older Adult*; and the title mentioned above, *The Puritans on How to Care for the Sick and Dying: A Contemporary Guide for Pastors and Counselors*. These books provide more specific advice. Nevertheless, some general practical principles may be offered, and the foremost is to seek counsel and guidance from your pastor as you make medical, legal, and funeral plans. "Where no counsel is, the people fall: but in the multitude of counsellors there is safety" (Prov. 11:14).

It is important to communicate one's desires for medical care to an appointed legal representative in case one becomes incapacitated. We do not want to burden others with futile care; neither do we want to cause our own murder! Written or verbal medical directives communicated to a legal representative will help to prevent such predicaments. Every Christian should "put his house in order," as the Westminster divines direct, by making a "will and testament" that provides for the disposition of one's temporal goods or estate after death and does so in a manner that glorifies God. It is wise to consult a lawyer to insure that your will meets the requirements of the law. Financial planners can help you with advice on how to conserve the value of your estate, avoid unnecessary duties or taxes, and provide for the payment of your debts, since we are required to "owe no man anything" (Rom. 13:8).

Finally, with the help of your pastor, make plans for your funeral and burial. In practical terms, it makes good financial sense to pre-pay for such things as embalming, coffins, vaults, and cemetery lots, since that will make the costs much lower. A written record of such plans makes it much easier for those who must put them into effect. Best of all, you can have a hand in making your funeral a God-glorifying occasion for preaching the gospel to others, especially to those you love most in this life. The Christian's funeral and coffin are a persuasive pulpit. The funeral is an excellent opportunity for a powerful exhortation to unbelieving family members and friends to flee to Christ for salvation, even as it provides comfort for grieving believers to rest in Christ's promises.[5]

---

5. Christians often wonder if cremation is a biblical practice, especially since it is a lot cheaper and laws require the safe disposal of human remains. While the Bible does not directly endorse or oppose cremation, it does provide examples of

A note of warning is in order. As pastors, lawyers, and funeral directors can all attest, nothing is worse than to leave such matters to be sorted out by those you leave behind when you die. The opportunities for uncertainty, confusion, crass disputes over who gets what, enduring family feuds, and costly legal battles are rife. It is far better to be guided by the general rules of God's Word, such as: "Let all things be done decently and in order" (1 Cor. 14:40); "Let all things be done unto edifying" (14:26); "Let all your things be done with charity [love]." (16:14); and "Do all to the glory of God" (10:31).

Conclusion: Dying Daily

Are you ready to die? Or, even more importantly: are you truly spiritually alive? If you are living in Christ, you are ready to die; though there are practical things that ought to be done, your house is essentially set in order. If you are not living in Christ, you are not ready to die. Dear friend, you must be ready; you must be born again. There is no other way to enter the kingdom of God. The Puritans used to say that the way to get ready to die is to practice dying while you are still physically alive—dying to yourself, dying to everything that would draw you away from Jesus Christ. Charles Spurgeon illustrates this well:

> No man would find it difficult [to die] who died every day. He would have practiced it so often that he would only have to die but once more; like the singer who has been through rehearsals, and is perfect for her part, and has but to pour out the notes once for all, and have done. Happy are they who every morning go down to Jordan's brink, and

---

burial. All of the major characters in the Bible, including Jesus, were interred and no one was cremated. While the dead body will decompose and eventually return to dust and ashes, for those at the graveside funeral service, there is a powerful image of the wages of sin as one gazes upon the full-body coffin and the hope of the resurrection of the reposed and "sleeping" body at the return of Christ—all of these are powerful biblical themes that are lessened by cremation. In light of these and additional factors, it seems to us that burial is by far the more biblical approach.

wade into the stream in fellowship with Christ, dying in the Lord's death, being crucified on his cross, and raised in his resurrection. They, when they shall climb their Pisgah, shall behold nothing but what has long been familiar to them, as they have studied the map of death.[6]

Perhaps you are not ready to die if you are still clinging to the empty toys and trinkets of this world. Perhaps you find your life in your friendships, your work, your possessions, your wealth, or your legalism; maybe, God forbid, some of you even live for sin. Whatever you live for, if Christ is not supreme, you are living for idols because you are putting those things above Him. You are not ready to die. In fact, you are not really living—but you could die at any moment! You are in an incredibly precarious and dangerous position. Meditate on the honest words of Robert Murray M'Cheyne, "If you die wrong the first time you cannot come back to die better a second time."[7]

The story is told of one of Spurgeon's good friends, Rowland Hill (1744–1833), a popular evangelical preacher who was quite discouraged during a certain season of his ministry due to what he judged to be a lack of saving fruit among his parishioners. One day he noticed a pig farmer walk by his house and into a slaughterhouse followed by dozens of his pigs. When the farmer came out of the slaughterhouse, Hill was there to query him: "How do you get these pigs to follow you to their physical death when I cannot get sinners to follow Christ to their eternal life?"

The farmer answered, "Did you not notice what I did as I walked along? Every few steps, I dropped a few crumbs of pig's food, and for those few crumbs, those pigs will follow me to their death."

Friend, do not be like those pigs. Do not be like the prodigal son, and follow this world for its pig food. Heed the advice of the

---

6. C. H. Spurgeon, "Dying Daily," sermon no. 828, on 1 Cor. 15:31, *Metropolitan Tabernacle Pulpit* (Pasadena, Tex.: Pilgrim Publications, 1976), 14:491.

7. Blanchard, *Complete Gathered Gold,* 137.

great Scottish theologian, Samuel Rutherford (1600–1661), who wrote, "Build your nest in no tree here [on earth], for God has sold the [entire] forest to death."[8] May God grant you to experience with the great ancient church father Augustine who could say of meditation upon death that "nothing has contributed more powerfully to wean me from all that held me down to earth."[9]

Seek heavenly food. Die daily to yourself, to your own righteousness, and to this world; live daily to Christ, and out of His righteousness. Do not rest until you can say, "For me to live is Christ, and to die is gain" (Phil. 1:21). Then you need not fear death, for you will be well prepared for this last enemy (1 Cor. 15:26). Why should you be afraid of death when you trust that, for Christ's sake, you will live forever by dying? As the Puritan commentator, Matthew Henry (1662–1714) said, "He whose head is in heaven need not fear to put his feet into the grave... It ought to be the business of every day to prepare for our last day."[10]

Spurgeon minces no words: "He who does not prepare for death is more than an ordinary fool. He is a madman."[11] Seek grace to live, therefore, as one prepared to die temporally, and to die as one prepared to live eternally.

---

8. Samuel Rutherford, letter of Jan. 15, 1629, to Lady Kenmure, in *Letters of Samuel Rutherford* (Edinburgh: Banner of Truth, 1984), 41.

9. Blanchard, *Complete Gathered Gold*, 131.

10. Blanchard, *Complete Gathered Gold*, 131, 139.

11. Blanchard, *Complete Gathered Gold*, 139.

DYING DEMONSTRATED
Faithful Perseverance until Death

James, a plump middle-aged man, was walking with his wife down the automotive aisle at a department store. All of a sudden he felt a fluttering in his chest and became short of breath; clasping his left breast with his right hand, he fell to the floor. His wife dropped to her knees by his side, yelling: "Help, help, someone call an ambulance!" Within seconds, people gathered around and a man nearby called "911" on his cell phone.

A nurse, who happened to be shopping, took charge of the situation. She knelt by James, who was now extremely pale, vigorously shook his shoulders in an attempt to arouse him, and placed two fingers on his neck to check for a pulse, lowering her ear to his mouth—"no pulse, no breathing, does anyone know CPR?" Looking directly at the man who phoned 911, she instructed him to go to the manager and ask for an "automatic external defibrillator" (AED).

A teenager standing in the aisle raised his hand, "I learned CPR for my lifeguard certification."

"Good," replied the nurse, "Begin chest compressions, and I will perform mouth-to-mouth."

"One, two, three…" the teen pressed forcefully on the middle of James's large chest.

Within ten minutes the Emergency Medical Service team arrived, and the paramedic took charge: "No pulse or breathing. Tom, ready the defibrillator. Hank, begin intubation. Sam, start a large bore IV. Did anyone witness the episode?"

James's wife spoke up, "He turned pale, clasped his chest, and fell to the floor."

"Ventricular fibrillation detected, sir," said Tom.

"Intubation complete, sir, I'm maintaining the airway with the Ambu Bag," Hank reported.

"18 gauge IV started in right antecubital area, sir," stated Sam.

"Good work," said the paramedic, "Shock with 200 joules after a countdown from three, then administer Epinephrine IV push. After the shock, continue ventilation; three, two, all clear, one, initiate shock."

James's body lifted briefly from the floor and flopped back down. "Normal sinus rhythm detected," replied Tom.

"Maintain the air way. Let's transport," said the paramedic, and James was taken to the local hospital, where he was admitted to the ICU and placed on a ventilator.

A couple of hours later, James's wife, his two sons, and his pastor were at the bedside, amidst the tangle of wires, tubing, air sounds, and beeping. The pastor prayed and offered words of consolation from Holy Scripture.

Forty-eight hours later, after a battery of diagnostic tests and examinations, the treating physician entered the room to explain what the studies revealed. "According to our testing," the doctor said, "it appears James had a sudden cardiac death episode, which means his heart beat really fast until it quivered, a condition referred to as ventricular fibrillation. The result is his heart stopped pumping blood to his brain and other organs. We were able to get his heart started again, but unfortunately, because of the span of time since his heart was not effectively beating and he had ceased breathing, he suffered irreversible damage to his brain. James is in a condition we refer to as total-brain failure or being brain-dead. Did he indicate his wishes if he was ever in this condition?"

Perseverance by Living Like Christ

Two months prior, James's pastor had preached a convicting and comforting sermon on Philippians 1:21: "For to me to live is Christ, and to die is gain." One of the applications of the exhortation was on how preparing ahead for medical crises and death was to live like Christ. "Jesus lived in such a way," said the pastor, "as to not place undue stress or unnecessary burdens on others; by God's grace, we should do everything in our power to do the same, especially when it comes to decisions we may not be able to make because we are incapacitated." Motivated by the sermon, James and his wife met with the pastor to discuss how to prepare more specifically for end-of-life issues. They talked about medical care from a biblical perspective, as well as drafting a living will, a last will and testament, and making funeral preparations. Over the course of a month, James and his wife arranged their end-of-life needs. James's wife replied to the doctor, "Yes, James indicated his wishes. He said if he was ever on life support and was diagnosed as brain-dead, he wanted to be kept comfortable and to have the life support withdrawn."

"Ok," said the doctor, "I will put in a referral for hospice care, and when everything is in place, we will withdraw the life support." After the hospice personnel arrived, medications were administered to prevent suffering and to calm his laborious attempts to breathe, and the breathing tube was withdrawn. With James's wife holding his hand, her two sons by her side, and their pastor present with a few close members from church, they sat together in peaceful silence resting in the promises of Jesus. About an hour later, James breathed his last, his soul was separated from his body, and he went into the presence of his faithful triune God in heaven.

The group, with tearful sorrow mixed with joy, reminisced about James's life. Soon the director from the funeral home arrived, James's body was released from the hospital, and the funeral home prepared him for burial. Three days later, about one hundred people were gathered at James's gravesite, and the pastor preached the sermon James had written notes on for his own funeral. The sermon was on Philippians 1:21 as well, but the sermon emphasized that to die is gain. The pastor waxed eloquent about the gains of dying with a living faith in Christ, how the saints were lifted to heaven in mystical communion, and how unbelievers were left on earth to feel the drawing pull of the dark-grave-hole of death. For several weeks after the funeral, the pastor met with James's wife and sons for grief support and counseling, while many in the congregation upheld them with continual prayer and practical acts of mercy.

Persevering in "Living Christ" to "Die Gain"

What did Paul mean when he wrote: "For to me to live is Christ, and to die is gain" (Phil. 1:21)?

What does it mean that Christ is our life and death our gain?

Since the Greek language does not have linking verbs, Paul literally says, "For me to live, *Christ*; to die, *gain.*" For Paul, Philippians 1:21 was his life. He is saying, as it were, "*Christ*—He is my life! And because I, by grace, live Christ, my death will be gain."

"For to me to live is Christ" means at least four things. First, when Christ is our life, we have a special *linkage* with Him. As theologians say, we are united to Him. This union with Christ is foundational for both real life and a peaceable death. We must be in Christ by faith. We must be justified by faith in Him, and out of that justification have a real relationship with Him. Our union with Him must result in communion with Him.

Second, it means we find our *life* in Christ. Then the aim of our daily life is to know Christ and to know Him better in His person, better in His natures, better in His offices, and better in sweet communion with Him. That is what theologians call sanctification: I want to become more holy in Christ. I want to know Him increasingly as my daily teaching Prophet, my daily interceding High Priest, and my daily ruling and guiding King. For a Christian, "to live is Christ" means that everything outside of Christ becomes death and everything connected with Christ becomes life.

Third, it means we *love* Christ. Paul could say that the love of Christ constrained him (2 Cor. 5:8–15). The love of Christ was Paul's great motivator which made him love Christ in return. It is what made him tick all day long. It filled his heart, his mouth, and his life. Every page of each of his New Testament letters is filled with Christ. Luther put it well when he said, "Paul could not keep Christ out of his pen because the Holy Spirit kept Christ in his heart."

Finally, "to live is Christ" is to grow in *likeness* to Christ. There was a savor of Christ that wafted out of Paul (2 Cor. 2:15). The fruits of Christ are the fruit of the Spirit: love, joy, peace, patience, kindness, etc. (Gal. 5:22–23), all of which are the moral profile of Christ. When Christ is our life, we become more like Him in developing a servant heart to serve God and others, a loving heart to really care about all kinds of people, and a humble heart to become more meek and lowly like our Savior.

In a word, when our life is Christ, our death will be *gain*. Every true Christian gains immediately by death (1) perfect freedom from all inclinations to sin and from all actual sins (Eph. 5:27; Rev. 14:5); (2) perfect freedom from all temptations to sin (Eph. 6:16; 1 Cor. 10:2; 2 Cor. 13:1); (3) perfect freedom from all the sorrows and miseries of this life (Job 14:1ff.; Prov. 23:5; Rev. 21:4); (4) perfect freedom from the hindrances of one's body (2 Cor. 15:43, 44, 49; Phil. 3:21); and (5) perfect freedom from all spiritual ignorance, being made perfect in the knowledge of God (Job 37:19; 1 Cor. 13:8–12). But there is more: the true Christian gains a perfect vision of God with all the joy and blessedness that vision gives (Matt. 5:8; John 17:24; 1 John 3:2). He gains access to the most blessed and delightful fellowship possible (Heb. 12:22, 23) and gains inconceivable joy (Ps. 16:11; Rev. 19:1). And all of these advantages will be eternal and everlasting (1 Pet. 1:3, 5).

In short, death will be gain because of what we leave behind and because of what we receive. Dear believer, imagine leaving behind your body of sin and death. Imagine no more having to confess, "Evil is present with me" (Rom. 7:21). No more sin—what a glorious thought! And then, no more buffeting Satan, no more enticing world—no more problems with the lust of the eye, the lust of the flesh, or the pride of life. No more unanswered prayers; no more vexing riddles. No more old nature to contend with! No more tears, no more pain, no more night, no more death, no more curse! To die is gain because of what I leave behind.

But death is also gain because of what I receive. Dying brings us into communion with Christ's sufferings. Dying gives us a unique experience of Christ's all-sufficient grace. Dying transforms us into Christ's image. Dying is our last and perhaps greatest opportunity to witness for Christ's glory. Dying brings us into Christ's presence—into intimate communion with Him, yes, into perfect eternal life with Him and perfect and yet cumulative knowledge of Him, ever knowing Him more fully to all eternity. Dying initiates us into heaven's perfect activities. We will worship and serve God perfectly. We will have perfect fellowship with the saints and angels in glory.

But if Christ is not your life, your death will not be gain. Your death will be a tragedy. Your death will lead you to hell to live forever apart from God's favor and under His wrath.

But for you, dear believer, death cannot harm you. It will only do you good; it will take you higher and further than the Bible, prayer, the sacraments, worship, and all the spiritual disciplines could ever take you in this life. It will take you right into the beatific vision of your glorious Savior. A sense of this sweet communion with Christ enabled the Puritan Thomas Goodwin to say in the midst of physical discomfort on his deathbed, "Ah! Is this dying? How have I dreaded as an enemy this smiling friend!"[1]

Such sweetness in dying is still often granted God's people today. For your encouragement, let me (Joel Beeke) share with you a few cases in my ministry:

Helen Staal was a dear child of God who lived Christ. She was one of the happiest Christians I have ever known, even as she had to

---

1. Blanchard, *Complete Gathered Gold*, 131.

endure more afflictions than nearly any person I have ever known. Over a few decades she was hospitalized around eighty times for a variety of illnesses, including cancer which eventually went to her brain. For a while, various medicines, as well as chemotherapy and radiation treatments seemed to work well for her, but eventually she could feel that the Lord was calling her home. Her mind began to be impacted and she knew it. One day she told me, "If I speak foolish things that make no sense to you, just ignore me; but I want you to know that since Jesus has been my all in my life, He will also be my all in my death, so when I talk about Him my mind will be clear to the end." And that is exactly what happened: whenever she spoke about Jesus, her mind was clear until her death!

Esther VanGiessen was another joyful Christian whom I was privileged to pastor for many years. She once told me that she had been given grace to trust Christ no matter how she might die, but she only hoped that she would not have to die as her mother had died—from a very painful form of pancreatic cancer. In God's inscrutable sovereignty, she was diagnosed with the same kind of pancreatic cancer. Instead of rebelling, she was sweetly submissive. Over a period of a few years she went through various treatments, and as with Helen, they were helpful for a while. But before long, death made its inroads and then appeared imminent. Her faith in Christ remained strong throughout the entire period except one night when her husband called me at 3:00 a.m. to come over as she felt deserted by God. What an unforgettable visit that was— God used His word to bring her out of that horrible pit and for the remainder of her earthly journey she testified at every visit of the goodness of Christ. Near the end, she underwent one more surgery. I was the last to see her, just before she was rolled away. Never will I forget her last words to me. I asked, "Esther, how are you doing? Is Christ still near to you?" She grasped my hand firmly, looked me straight in the eyes, and then spoke with overwhelming conviction, emphasizing each word: "*Whether we live, we live unto the Lord; and whether we die, we die unto the Lord: whether we live therefore, or die, we are the Lord's*" (Rom. 14:8). She went home to be with the Lord shortly thereafter.

Those who live well—persevering in finding their life in Christ—usually die well, clinging to Christ. The Puritan Richard Sibbes (1577–1635), often nicknamed "the heavenly Doctor" for his godly, Christ-centered life, confessed as death drew near, "Through Christ death is become friendly to me." And John Newton (1725–1807), author of the famous hymn "Amazing Grace," said on his deathbed, "I am packed, sealed and waiting for the post [of death]."[2] Pray that God will help you live Christ so that you may gain in dying!

---

2. Blanchard, *Complete Gathered Gold*, 132.

12

DYING DELIGHTFULLY
Victorious Death

Our lives are not just a journey to death. They are a journey to one of two eternal places: heaven or hell. In heaven all evil is walled out and all good is walled in. Heaven is an eternal day that knows no sunset. Hell is an eternal night that knows no sunrise. Which destination are you heading for? Are you a true Christian—a follower of Jesus Christ? Do you trust only in the doing and dying of Jesus—in His active and passive obedience—as your ground of acceptance with God? If you were arrested today for being a Christian, would there be enough evidence to convict you? Are you born again, justified by gracious faith alone, and on the narrow path to the Celestial City?

If so, you may have every hope that your death will be victorious; that, despite the discomfort and pain of the misery associated with dying, you may die joyfully and delightfully by looking to Jesus, the author and finisher of your faith, resting in justification by faith alone in Christ alone to the glory of God alone. As Paul put it, "We…rejoice in hope of the glory of God" (Rom. 5:2).

Dear believer, when we die, then "there shall be no more death" (Rev. 21:4). You will ascend triumphantly, gloriously, majestically, peacefully, and joyfully into the heaven of heavens, where you will be a blessed part of one undivided body of Christ and His church (see John 17). There Christ will present you as His bride to His Father without spot or wrinkle in soul or body to be permanently instated into heaven to dwell forever with your precious Lamb: "For the Lamb which is in the midst of the throne shall feed them, and shall lead them unto living fountains of waters: and God shall wipe away all tears from their eyes" (Rev. 7:17).

You will be in tearless glory living with Christ forever, crying out, "Worthy is the Lamb!" You will drink of the fountains of the full enjoyment of God, praising Him for all eternity in the most holy, glorious, and perfect activities: worshipping God, resting in Him, praising Him in song, serving Him forever in His temple, exercising authority with Him, and above all, gazing upon the face of Jesus while communing with Him, and enjoying loving the triune God more fully than ever. You will be communing with the holy angels and redeemed saints made perfect (cf. Luke 18:7; Rev. 6:9–11). Delightful, victorious, holy, happy, eternal day when we shall ever be with the Lord—sin-free in Immanuel's land, ever growing in our capacity and fullness of knowing and relishing Him!

Examples of Victorious Death

God gives dying grace to His people for death's hour. Some of His people die with little fanfare. They depart this life quietly, serenely, with barely a sigh. For others, the king of terrors is more violent, but Jesus brings them through in the end and gives them the victory. Still others receive special measures of dying grace, so that their deathbeds become their best pulpits. Such was the case with the well-known Scottish theologian, Thomas Halyburton (1674–1712), who died at the age of thirty-seven. To read in his *Memoirs* the nearly seventy pages of his last sayings, which were recorded by those around his deathbed, is to dwell in the vestibule of heaven. Here is only one example: "Come, sweet Lord Jesus, receive this spirit, fluttering within my breast like a bird to be out of a snare. I wait for thy salvation as the watchman watcheth for the morning. I am weary with delays. I faint for thy salvation. Why are His chariot wheels so long a coming?"[1]

---

1. *Memoirs of Thomas Halyburton*, ed. Joel R. Beeke (Grand Rapids: Reformation Heritage Books, 1996), 266–67.

History is full of tens of thousands of saints who have died victoriously in Jesus with great joy, despite the affliction death brought. Biblical examples, such as those of Paul (2 Tim. 4:6–8) and Stephen (Acts 7:54–60), are well known. So are the cases of many martyrs, such as John Huss (1369–1415), Hugh Latimer (c. 1486–1555) and Nicholas Ridley (c. 1500–1555), and repentant Thomas Cranmer (1489–1556). Cranmer recanted under pressure from Roman Catholic Queen Mary (1516–1558), but he recanted his recantation, went to the stake, and as the flames crept up his body, he stretched his right hand into the midst of the flames, and cried out: "This hand hath offended"—and died horrifically but victoriously!

One of my (Joel Beeke) favorite simple accounts of a victorious death is that of a Scotsman, David Dickson (c. 1583–1662), well-known for writing the first commentary on the Westminster Confession of Faith and for his commentaries on the Psalms, Matthew, and Hebrews. When his friends were gathered around his deathbed, one of them asked him when in the throes of a painful death what he was thinking. Dickson replied, "I have taken all my bad deeds and put them on a heap, and I have taken my good deeds as well, and I have put them on the same heap. And I have run away from that heap into the arms of Jesus. I die in peace."[2]

Still others have written helpfully about dying and death. Affliction was a life-long companion to Puritan pastor, Richard Baxter (1615–1691). He wrote a 700-page classic, *The Saints' Everlasting Rest,* while suffering from tuberculosis (a severe respiratory disease with long-term debilitating effects), chronic pain, and the frequent prospect of dying. In this condition, Baxter looked death in the face and experienced the sufficient grace of God to sustain him until he fell asleep in Jesus in 1691.

Baxter impresses upon his readers that suffering, sickness, and death are to be expected in this life; they are the norm at present. According to Baxter, these miseries remind Christians they are not

---

2. Joel R. Beeke and Randall J. Pederson, *Meet the Puritans* (Grand Rapids: Reformation Heritage Books, 2006), 668–72.

to seek physical comfort, rest, and healing here and now so much as we are to seek to know Christ better. He says that when we are "fastened to [our] beds with pining sickness, the world is nothing, and heaven is something." Further, he writes:

> O healthful sickness! O comfortable sorrows! O gainful losses! O enriching poverty! O blessed day that ever I was afflicted! Not only the green pastures and still waters, but the rod and staff, they comfort us. Though the word and Spirit do the main work, yet suffering so unbolts the door of the heart, that his word has an easier entrance.

Baxter describes disease, dying, and facing death as providential means God uses to permit "easier entrance" of the Spirit-blessed Word into the human heart, so that it may transform us and enable us to rejoice in the midst of sorrow. Contrary to the twenty-first-century mindset that sees suffering as worthless and meaningless, dying, death, and all of the misery they contain are full of significance. All of them point to the reality of the ultimate problem the entire human race faces, namely, sin, and to its only solution, faith and hope in the life and death of Jesus Christ, His resurrection from the dead, and His return from heaven with "healing in his wings" (Mal. 4:2).

Victory over the Pale Horse

God often uses the "pale horse" of the apocalypse, whose rider's "name...was Death" (Rev. 6:8), as a providential instrument to strip His people of self-reliance and to drive them to dependence on the person and work of Jesus Christ via the means of grace. The Christian has victory over spiritual and everlasting death and someday physical healing, rest, and comfort will come, but at present dying is inevitable; everyone will pass from dying into a state of physical death, unless the Lord returns in our lifetime to bring history to an end.

Double graces, natural and supernatural, flow from the hand of God to Christians in this experience of dying and death. The Christian has the common grace benefit of medical science at his or her disposal. As with all such benefits, however, there are limits to their usefulness. Nevertheless, there are no limits to the benefits of the special grace of God in Christ, dispensed in the means of grace, namely, the ministry of the Word, the sacraments, the communion of the saints, praise and prayer. Through diligent use of these means, Christians obtain help, comfort, strength, and hope in order to tread the path of dying, confront Death riding his pale horse, and to die delightfully in Jesus:

> The LORD is the portion of mine inheritance and of my cup: thou maintainest my lot. The lines are fallen unto me in pleasant places; yea, I have a goodly heritage. I will bless the LORD, who hath given me counsel: my reins also instruct me in the night seasons. I have set the LORD always before me: because he is at my right hand, I shall not be moved. Therefore my heart is glad, and my glory rejoiceth: my flesh also shall rest in hope. For thou wilt not leave my soul in hell; neither wilt thou suffer thine Holy One to see corruption. Thou wilt shew me the path of life: in thy presence is fulness of joy; at thy right hand there are pleasures for evermore. (Ps. 16:5–11)

"Precious in the sight of the LORD is the death of his saints" (Ps. 116:15).

At Home with the Shepherd

David concludes his magnificent twenty-third Psalm with his eyes on the future: "I will dwell in the house of the LORD for ever." "The house of the LORD" is a biblical expression intimating the place where God dwells with His people, whether in the tabernacle, the temple, the church, or ultimately in heaven.[3]

Oh, how blessed is a believer's translation from the church on earth to the church in heaven! Goodness and mercy have followed him throughout life, and now goodness and mercy surround him on every side. Who shall describe the unspeakable joy of his soul as he enters into glory? How satisfied he will be with all he sees and hears! With grateful adoration he will worship his faithful God who has fulfilled all His promises and surpassed even the believer's highest expectations. Who can conceive of the joy and gratitude with which he will join in the song of his redeemed brethren: "Unto him that loved us, and washed us from our sins in his own blood, and hath made us kings and priests unto God and his Father; to him be glory and dominion for ever and ever. Amen" (Rev. 1:5–6).

The soul in heaven dwells in a perfected state. It can do no wrong, see no iniquity, hear no evil, and receive no spiritual harm. The Redeemer, now seen in His glorified human form, fills the believer's thoughts, is the theme of the soul's conversations, and is the object of the soul's adoration. The soul burns within itself while Christ reveals what He has suffered and the glory that is now His. It experiences inexpressible delight in Christ's presence and praises Him in high, holy, and celestial strains.

How imperfect are our highest conceptions of the beauty, blessedness, holiness, and glory of God's eternal house. To know it as it is, we would have to be caught up, as Paul was, into the "third heaven" but even then its realities cannot be described in earthly language (2 Cor. 12:2, 4). As great as is the delight and glory that the departed saint enjoys in his best spiritual condition, there is more to come. His mortal body will be raised out of the dust and no longer be natural and corruptible, but will be transformed into a Spirit-dominated and immortal body, made fit for heaven (1 Cor. 15:44).

---

3. Among the almost three hundred texts using the expression "house of the Lord" or "house of God," see Gen. 28:17; Exod. 23:19; 2 Chron. 3:1; Pss. 42:4; 122:1; Mic. 4:1; 1 Tim. 3:15; Heb. 10:21; 1 Pet. 4:17.

Gathered from the dust of the grave by the hand of the Creator, it will become a pure and crystal vessel prepared to receive the believer's glorified soul. Joy, delight, and a sense of ultimate victory will abound in the house of the Lord on resurrection morning, when the souls of the saints are joined with their resurrected, glorified bodies. They will be delivered from the bondage of corruption and be introduced into the glorious liberty of the children of God (Rom. 8:21). "So shall we ever be with the Lord" (1 Thess. 4:17).

When the Great Shepherd appears in the heavens, there will be joy unequalled in heaven and earth. The "times of restitution of all things" will gladden all the holy angels and every redeemed human being (Acts 3:21). The trumpet will sound to proclaim that "the year of my redeemed is come" (Isa. 63:4). Universal liberty will be granted to all God's elect. There will be a continuous season of spiritual peace, delight, joy, and love. All the saints will be arrayed in white and shining garments; as victors; they will wave palm branches and wear crowns of life and righteousness received from the hand of Christ.

The dead in Christ will rise first, and the saints who are still alive will be changed into the likeness of their Lord. Their vile bodies will also be changed into the likeness of His glorious body—incorruptible, powerful, spiritual, and heavenly (Phil. 3:21; 1 Cor. 15:42–44, 49). Then in one blessed company they will all be caught up in the air to meet their glorious Redeemer (1 Thess. 4:13–18). In soul and body the redeemed saints will now be the perfect possession of their Lord. Their names will be confessed before the angels of God (Luke 12:8), and they will possess their everlasting inheritance. They will forever dwell in the house of the Lord and surround the throne of the Lamb!

The pilgrims will rest in their true home (Heb. 11:13). As good and faithful servants, they have completed their work, which the Lord declares to be well done. They are then invited to enter into their Master's joy (Matt. 25:21). The runners of the race have finished their course and have won the prize of their high calling (Phil. 3:14; 2 Tim. 4:7). The soldiers of Christ have fought the good fight

of faith, secured victory by grace, and received the crown of righteousness (2 Tim. 4:7–8).

The little flock of sheep need not fear anymore, for they see that
their Father's good pleasure was to give them the kingdom (Luke
12:32). They were poor but now find treasure in heaven, inheritance
in light, fullness of joy, and an eternal weight of glory (Matt. 6:20;
2 Cor. 4:17). All doubts of their acceptance are gone. Faith has given
way to sight; hope has given way to fruition. They see that the One
who went before them has indeed prepared a place for them (John
14:2). They are safe within their fold. They are welcomed at the table
that their gracious Host has prepared for them. They behold the
King in His beauty (Isa. 33:17) and live in the enjoyment of His
victorious love. The Lord God Almighty is their unfading portion,
their ever-open temple, their everlasting light, and their eternal
glory (Rev. 21: 22–23). They dwell in the house of the Lord and are
forever blessed because they are surrounded by the triune God.

Conclusion

Jesus says, "Surely I come quickly." And the bride says, "Even so,
come, Lord Jesus" (Rev. 22:20). Given that the best is yet to be, God's
people often long to be with Christ who is their life. Like Paul, they
thank God that not even death can separate them from the love of
God in Christ Jesus their Lord (Rom. 8:38–39). In fact, death unites
them all the more closely to Christ and His blessings by bringing
them into their more full and permanent possession of the riches
of heaven.

The Puritans used to say that the day of their death was better
than their wedding day. Thomas Brooks (1608–1680) confessed, "A
believer's last day is his best day."[4] "Death is the funeral of all our
sorrows," said Watson.[5] Sibbes put it this way: "Death is not now
the death of me, but death will be the death of my misery, the death

---

4. Blanchard, *Complete Gathered Gold*, 132.

5. Blanchard, *Complete Gathered Gold*, 134.

of my sins; it will be the death of my corruptions. But death will be my birthday in regard of happiness. Death is only a grim porter to let us into a stately palace.... Shall I be afraid to die, when in death I commend my soul to such a sweet Lord, and go to my Husband and to my King?"[6] The great eighteenth-century itinerant evangelist George Whitefield (1714–1770) prayed, "Lord, keep me from a sinful and too eager desire after death. I desire not to be impatient. I wish quietly to wait till my blessed change comes."[7]

For many of our Reformed and Puritan forebears, death spelled victory. For them, death did not extinguish the light, but it merely put out the lamp because the eternal dawn has come. We die to die no more, for in and through Christ, death brings life and perfect and complete victory in its wake—*forever*!

---

6. Blanchard, *Complete Gathered Gold,* 133, 136.
7. Blanchard, *Complete Gathered Gold,* 132.

Further Reading

Where to Start

Christopher W. Bogosh, *Healing Hope: Restoring the Superiority of the Christian Hope*

Christopher W. Bogosh, *The Golden Years: Healthy Aging and the Older Adult*

Christopher W. Bogosh, *Going to Jesus: What to Expect when Facing Death*

Thomas Boston, *Human Nature in Its Fourfold State*

Ligon Duncan, *Fear Not! Death and the Afterlife from a Christian Perspective*

Paul Helm, *The Last Things: Death, Judgment, Heaven and Hell*

John R. Ling, *Responding to the Culture of Death—A Primer of Bioethical Issues*

Al Martin, *Grieving, Hope and Solace: When a Loved One Dies in Christ*

Gary P. Stewart, et al. *Basic Questions on End of Life Decisions: How Do We Know What's Right?*

Joni Tada, *When Is It Right to Die? Suicide, Euthanasia, Suffering, Mercy*

Douglas Taylor, *I Shall Not Die, But Live*

In More Detail

Richard Baxter, *The Saints' Everlasting Rest*

Christopher W. Bogosh, *Biblical Medicine: Developing a Christian Worldview for Medical Science*

Christopher W. Bogosh, *The Puritans on How to Care for the Sick and Dying: A Contemporary Guide for Pastors and Counselors*

Christopher W. Bogosh, *Compassionate Jesus: Rethinking the Christian's Approach to Modern Medicine*

Zacharie Boyd, *The Last Battle of the Soul in Death*

George Burgess, *The Last Enemy: Conquering and Conquered*

Bill Davis, *Departing in Peace: Biblical Decision-Making at the End of Life*

William Dodd, *Reflections on Death*

Charles Drelincourt, *The Christian's Defence against the Fears of Death: With Seasonable Directions How to Prepare Ourselves to Die Well*

John F. Kilner, Arlene B. Miller, and Edmund D. Pellegrino, eds., *Dignity and Dying: A Christian Appraisal*

John R. Ling, *The Edge of Life: Dying, Death and Euthanasia*

Rob Moll, *The Art of Dying: Living Fully into the Life to Come*

William Sherlock, *A Practical Discourse Concerning Death*

The Bigger Picture

Christopher W. Bogosh, *Modern Medicine's Definition of Death: Ethical Implications for Christians*

Robert Bolton, *The Four Last Things: Death, Judgment, Hell, and Heaven*

John W. Cooper, *Body, Soul, and Life Everlasting: Biblical Anthropology and the Monism-Dualism Debate*

John Frame, *Medical Ethics: Principles, Persons, and Problems*

David Clyde Jones, *Biblical Christian Ethics*

Terrence Nichols, *Death and Afterlife: A Theological Introduction*

Sherwin B. Nutland, *How We Die: Reflections on Life's Final Chapter*

Robert D. Orr, *Medical Ethics and the Faith Factor: A Handbook for Clergy and Health-Care Professionals*

David E. Stannard, *The Puritan Way of Death: A Study in Religion, Culture, and Social Change*

Elizabeth C. Tingle and Jonathan Willis, eds., *Dying, Death, Burial and Commemoration in Reformation Europe*

David VanDrunen, *Bioethics and the Christian Life: A Guide to Making Difficult Decisions*

Christopher P. Vogt, *Patience, Compassion, Hope, and the Christian Art of Dying Well*